WHO SHOULD READ THIS BOOK?

This book was written for **supervisors** at any stage of their career who may be struggling with the people-side of the work. Supervisors in any organization can benefit from learning these 10 common-sense lessons.

Anyone transitioning to a leadership position at the supervisory level in manufacturing, those just starting out in their careers, or those planning a long-term career who need to build their people skills will benefit from the practical lessons shared in this book. Managers who are accountable for supervisors who are struggling to manage their teams might also take-away insight about struggles facing supervisors who are promoted from within based on their technical skills, who might be lacking in interpersonal skills.

More **experienced supervisors, managers, and others** might also benefit from reading this book, or by reading "Lean on Civility" which addresses in a more formal way critical communication strategies and how to implement them. Strategies in Lean on Civility include the Masotti Feedback Method, AEIOU strategy, The Civility Continuum, and much more.

For those who might have already assessed skills gaps in these critical "soft" communication and interpersonal areas, consider contacting events@civilityexperts.com for details about **our online and live delivery workshops, *Civility - a Continuous Improvement Strategy.*** And if you need help assessing your teams' skills in civility competency areas, we can help with that too. Visit www.civilityexperts.com and take the **no-fee online Civility Culture Compass Assessment**.

Social Competence for Manufacturing Supervisors
Three Phones and a Radio

By Christian Masotti

©Propriety Publishing
All Rights Reserved 2020

Table of Contents

Introduction..5
Acknowledgment...15
Dedication...16
How to Use This Book...17
About Christian Masotti...20
Social Competence for Manufacturing Supervisors –
    Background..21
Rationale and Supports for the Book..........................22
About Lewena Bayer- Contributor...............................24
Lessons and Social Competence Strategies Summary
    Chart...25
Chapter 1: Wait for it!..29
Chapter 2: Just Be Nice!...42
Chapter 3: Don't Be the Donut and Clipboard Guy.....56
Chapter 4: Listen to Wise Old Men and Women.........68
Chapter 5: ALWAYS Tell the Truth..............................80
Chapter 6: Tell Me What You Want (What You Really,
    Really Want)...96
Chapter 7: It Will Only Hurt for a Minute...................110
Chapter 8: Actually, I Know Absolutely Nothing About
    Trains..122
Chapter 9: Be a Strong Competitor...........................133
Chapter 10: You Are Exactly Where You Want To Be.........144
Chapter 11: Sources and Resources........................152

Introduction
Start Here

Here, after 20+ years in a range of supervisory positions, are a few things I know for sure:

- It does not matter whether you are assembling cars, converting a hockey arena to a concert venue, painting parts, bottling wine, fixing trains, or making steel, as a supervisor in any manufacturing environment, **you do not need to know everything about whatever it is you are doing**, manufacturing or producing. **But, if you do not know everything about the products and processes where you work, you had better be humble enough to acknowledge this, and you better be open to learning ongoing and learning from others**. (Chapter 4)

- It does not matter whether you are old, young, male, female, new or on the job for 15 years, charismatic, good looking, rich, poor, educated, overweight, smoke, don't smoke, are a person of culture, or somehow different than the people you work with, **at the end of the day, people will remember how you make them feel.** In real life at work, most people just want to feel valued, trusted, and respected. If you can achieve this and be perceived as a decent human being – most other attributes account for very little. (Chapter 2)

- It does not matter what people say. People say all kinds of things for all kinds of reasons and you can't put a lot of stock into words. However, **how a person acts, usually tells you what he/she really thinks**, what his/her values are, and who he/she is as a person. (Chapter 10)

- It does not matter how much you think you know, **"*collaboration is currency in the new world of work*"** (L Bayer). An essential aspect of supervising is collaboration, and to be a good collaborator you need to consistently and consciously exhibit civility. I have learned that Civility is a continuous improvement strategy for building strong interpersonal relationships at work. (Chapter 8)

When I first started out in manufacturing, and through my experiences in different types of organizations over the years, including supervising conversions in sports venues, coaching small business entrepreneurs, teaching civility, etc. I have realized that many people moving into, or aspiring to acquire, supervisory positions never learn the seemingly simple lessons I've mentioned above. This is due in large part to the fact that they simply do not have the social competence they need to be successful in a supervisory role.

For our purposes in this book, "social competence" refers to **the ability to handle social interactions effectively. In other words, social competence refers to getting along well with others, being able to form and maintain close relationships, and responding in adaptive ways in social settings**[1]. Social competence is made up of emotional, social, cognitive, and behavioural skills and is primarily exhibited through effective communication and the ability to build rapport and trust.

Over time I've learned some important lessons related to this social aspect of success. Ten (10) of these lessons are captured in this book. Four (4) of them are highlighted above.

---

[1] https://www.researchgate.net/publication/319588343_Social_Competence

> *"Common sense is not common practice, and when it comes to civility, you cannot make the mistake of assuming people know - or will do - the right and good thing."* L. Bayer, CEO Civility Experts Inc.

While I would say that on the surface many of these lessons might seem like common sense, I have experienced, as quoted above by my colleague Lew Bayer, CEO Civility Experts Inc., it is often the simple things that we take for granted. When we find ourselves in new or challenging positions, have low topical knowledge, have something to prove, or are ego-focused, many of us don't start with what is obvious and simple. Instead, we unwittingly choose the hard way.

Learning and applying these simple common-sense social competence strategies can be of tremendous benefit. For example, applying these lessons has enabled me to:

- Build strong working relationships
- Earn a reputation for being civil and credible
- Acquire all kinds of varied opportunities in manufacturing as well as other fields
- Learn continuously
- Achieve success as a supervisor and leader in the field
- Apply what I have learned in manufacturing in my life and in work unrelated to manufacturing

Social skills are critical for supervisors because the role of supervisor is a people-focused job. This book has been devised for manufacturing supervisors specifically, but I would suggest that these 10 common sense communication lessons and corresponding strategies could easily be applied to supervisors in any industry.

In manufacturing, the supervisor role is distinct from a manager's role which is typically focused on setting production goals and managing production processes.

In theory, this is not unlike other industries. Basically, supervisors are responsible for the day-to-day supervision of the personnel whose job it is to physically run the production processes in all types of manufacturing operations.

Supervisors are tasked with ensuring that targets are met, and this is achieved by making sure that the production lines run smoothly. Similar expectations would apply to hospitality or sales environments, and even academic organizations whereas for example the supervisor, who may be called something else, reports to a person higher up who is accountable for setting policy and decision-making, where the supervisor is responsible for supervising the day to day activities of a team.

In manufacturing, where the bulk of my experience lies, supervisors are responsible for the people side of production. In doing their jobs effectively, supervisors also manage performance, quality, efficiencies, costs, and safety.

Interestingly though, typical manufacturing job descriptions for supervisors, (see sample in Chapter 15) and the associated on-the-job training tend to focus more on the data collection and process-oriented tasks that supervisors are responsible for, and the social and interpersonal skill components are glossed over. This is problematic as it often results in putting people who have strong technical skills, but underdeveloped people skills, in positions where people skills are essential. Because most of us tend to default to our comfort zones or where our strengths lie when we are tired or under pressure, the environment in most manufacturing organizations, in fact, inhibits the development of these critical "soft" skills.

A recent study by ACT[2] focusing on manufacturing supervisors supports this point. Results on jobs from 98 manufacturing companies were analyzed, yielding a total of

---

[2] https://www.industryweek.com/the-economy/public-policy/article/21935878/consider-this-what-do-manufacturing-supervisors-really-do-on-the-job

4,768 tasks (many of which were overlapping from company to company), this was done to determine what supervisors actually do on the job. So, what do they do?

Researchers identified 12 major categories of tasks that manufacturing supervisors perform. According to those who are employed as manufacturing supervisors, the task categories below are listed in rank order by the frequency of their occurrence across jobs and tasks.

Supervisors spend significant time monitoring to:

1) Ensure safety
2) Ensure product quality
3) Evaluate and improve work processes.

In close concert with their monitoring roles, supervisors also spend time

4) "Being the expert,"
5) Mastering and maintaining specialized tools required for the job; and troubleshooting machine and work environment issues and resolving problems

Supervisors also manage production

6) By receiving direction and orders from management or customers;
7) Preparing detailed work assignments
8) Managing production levels to meet goals

So, that's eight of the 12 critical tasks –we are three-quarters of the way through the list. Have you noticed the missing element? Researchers were surprised to see no mention to this point of the interpersonal relationships associated with the management of people. Remember, this list of tasks came directly from the job incumbents -- those actually performing the tasks each day.

The last four task categories did reflect the interpersonal side of managing people and relationships. These range from:

9) Handling relationships with employees through using good communication skills and team development
10) Providing feedback, coaching, and training for those they supervise; to managing other relationships
11) Using good management communication skills and providing timely management reporting
12) Building solid rapport and relationships with internal and external customers

Wouldn't it make sense, that if the core purpose of the supervisor role is to manage people, that tasks 9-12 would be charted as top priority versus being at the end of the list? And what does it say about the culture of manufacturing, where clearly the production workers are critical to the success of the organization, that tasks related to building morale, trust, feedback, communication, relationship building, and rapport are at the bottom of the list?

Isn't it odd that supervisors are only spending an estimated 1/3 of their time on the people-oriented tasks? Shouldn't the bulk of their time be focused on the employees they are supervising?

What would happen if we reversed the order of priority? If supervisors spent 2/3 of their time on tasks 6-12, e.g., focused on building relationships, coaching on the job, giving meaningful feedback, monitoring, and measuring behaviour and activities?

Wouldn't this approach empower the people on the floor to take responsibility for the first 5 tasks outlined on the list above? Shouldn't production employees be focused on safety and being "experts" in their niche, maintaining specialized tools, concerned about quality etc.? Wouldn't making this change free up time for supervisors to actually supervise?

Why is the focus on the process-oriented tasks? In my experience this happens for three reasons:

a) Supervisors really don't understand what their job is – that is, the workplace culture has been built around long-term employees who have strong technical skills and find themselves in supervisory and/or management positions. For these supervisors, it is easier (and likely habit) to do what they know and so they end up being very skilled production workers who just happen to have a supervisor title.
b) Supervisors know what they are supposed to do with regard to the people side of the job - but they are not skilled in this area, and so default to their comfort skill area which is completing process-oriented tasks.
c) A "just do what you're told", autocratic, demanding, and frequently uncivil communication approach has become embedded in the organizational culture such that supervisors who might be inclined to take a new/better approach end up taking on the existing old-school approach that their manager uses and expects.

While most organizations do have onboarding programs and sometimes offer extensive training related to the products and processes, very little training is done in the area of people skills. The things supervisors *really* need to know relate to people. This includes managing the social aspects of things. Supervisors need to have high "social acuity" – that is they need to have a keen social sense. They must be consistently accurate and timely in their perceptions and assessments of social nuances in a range of settings. They need to know how to:

- Read contextual cues
- Be attentive to the nuances of workplace culture
- Navigate politics in union environments
- Identify who will be an ally and who will be a challenge
- Build trust

- Repair when a trust is broken
- Consider contextual aspects when timing everything from greetings, to feedback, to workplace coaching, and performance reviews
- Communicate in a way that leaves everyone involved in the interaction feeling valued
- Acknowledge differences that make a difference, e.g., related to gender, culture, generation
- Give timely and effective feedback
- Monitor and manage nonverbal cues to boost credibility and perceived competence
- Adapt a supervisory approach and style to meet the needs of individual workers
- Apply adult learning principles
- Maintain credibility as a leader but still be perceived as approachable by the production team

There is research suggesting that our general intelligence scores in many developed countries are on the decline[3]. And countless studies compiled by Civility Experts Inc. support the idea that Social Intelligence (as one of multiple intelligences) specifically has plummeted over the last two decades. This supports my experience that many supervisors and managers simply need more training when it comes to the social aspect of supervising people. There is a growing body of research validating this view.

As one example, in a Forbes article titled, *7 Leadership Skills Most Managers Lack*[4], Liz Ryan, states, "we are starting to tell the truth about the fact that most people in leadership positions are lacking in critical skills. They don't know how to talk to their employees and they don't know how to listen.

---

[3] https://www.nbcnews.com/think/opinion/iq-rates-are-dropping-many-developed-countries-doesn-t-bode-ncna1008576

[4] https://www.forbes.com/sites/lizryan/2016/05/26/seven-leadership-skills-most-managers-lack/#ed850867ebb3

If they received any management training at all, they were probably trained to dole out work assignments and evaluate people. They don't know how to probe for understanding or how to create cohesion on a team"

This book presents an opportunity for me to share insights such as those listed above along with best practices that I have learned on the job – often the hard way. It is my hope that new, young, and maybe even a few veteran supervisors, will benefit from learning strategies that helped me succeed in what can be an incredibly stressful, physically demanding, and unkind industry.

Who Should Read This Book?

This book was written for **supervisors** at any stage of their career who may be struggling with the people-side of the work. While the focus is on manufacturing environments, supervisors in any organization can benefit by learning these 10 commonsense lessons.

Anyone transitioning to a leadership position at the supervisory level in manufacturing, those just starting out in their careers, or those planning a long-term career in manufacturing who need to build their people skills will benefit from the practical lessons shared in this book. Managers who are accountable for supervisors who are struggling to manage their teams might also take-away insight about challenges facing supervisors who are promoted from within based on their technical skills, but who might be lacking in interpersonal skills.

More **experienced supervisors, managers, and others** will also benefit from reading this book, or by reading *Lean on Civility* which addresses in a more formal way critical communication strategies and how to implement them. Strategies in *Lean on Civility* include the Masotti Feedback Method, AEIOU strategy, The Civility Continuum, and much more.

For those who might have already assessed skills gaps in these critical "soft" communication and interpersonal areas, consider contacting **events@civilityexperts.com** for details about our **online and live delivery workshops,** *Civility – a Continuous Improvement Strategy.* And if you need help assessing your teams' skills in civility competency areas, we can help with that too. Visit **www.civilityexperts.com** and take the **no-fee online Civility Culture Compass Assessment.**

Acknowledgment

This book is for all the people I've worked with and grown up in the industry with, over the years, you know who you are. As first-time, front-line supervisors we figured it out together – the parts shortages, machine breakdowns, shipment delays, regulatory changes, chronic time constraints, physical demands, technology glitches, manpower issues…and so on. Manufacturing is one of those environments where what doesn't kill you makes you stronger and together we learned and struggled, and succeeded and celebrated. We built a community that supported and coached each other, and we survived.

My appreciation goes out to all of you who mentored and encouraged me over the years. Thank you for sharing your knowledge and successes with me. I hope you see some of your history and experiences in this book and that it will be a good resource for first-time front-line supervisors.

Dedication

To my sons Xavier and Sebastian who are now men starting out in their own careers, I am proud to be your father and hope aspects of my strong work ethic as well as the lessons I have learned and shared with you, will help you make good and right choices in your work and life. I love you.

How to Use This Book

This book is meant as a reference and resource for new supervisors. Each chapter includes:

- A key take-away: This is a lesson I learned on the job that I want to share with you
- General information about the communication skills and/or strategies you need to be able to learn this lesson
- A "how-to" that we refer to as a "Masotti Commonsense Social Competence Strategy" – a tried and tested technique for applying the lesson in a practical way
- Vocabulary
- Tools you can use to support your learning

Snapshot of the Book

Introduction – Start Here

Chapter 1 – Wait for It!
When you go into a situation with an open mind and you assume the best of people when you accept them on the surface without judgment, **people can surprise you** and it is equally surprising how much you can learn about yourself, and about others when you wait for it.

Chapter 2 – Just be Nice
At the end of the day, people will remember how you make them feel. In real life at work, most **people want to feel valued, trusted, and respected**. You can achieve this in large part just by being nice.

Chapter 3 – Don't be the Donut and Clipboard Guy
As a supervisor, you cannot hide out in your office and expect to be successful on the job. At some point, **you're going to have to engage with people**. Technology and paperwork

cannot replace the power of face-to-face interaction.

Chapter 4 – Listen to Wise Old Men and Women
If you are not the most experienced or the most educated person, you had better be humble enough to acknowledge this fact. And, **you had better be open to learning ongoing**, and to learning from others.

Chapter 5 – Always Tell the Truth
Consistent character will often outperform competence. This is because consistency of character builds trust. When you have trust, people will work with you. You don't have to be the smartest or the most skilled when you have the cooperation of your work team and you can benefit from the competency of the collective.

Chapter 6 – Tell me What You Want, What You Really, Really Want
If you actually pay attention, if you go into situations and interactions with the intention of being of service to someone, and you ask questions, and then **watch and listen**, **people will almost always tell you what they want**, even if they don't realize they are doing it.

Chapter 7 – It Will Only Hurt for a Minute
As a supervisor, you are going to have to look people in the eye and tell them the truth. You're going to have to discipline grown men and women, and some of them aren't going to like it. You are frequently not going to be the most popular person in the room and **occasionally your ego is going to take a punch. You're going to have to learn to bounce back and carry on.**

Chapter 8 – Collaboration is Currency
It does not matter how much you think you know, *"collaboration is currency in the new world of work"*. An essential aspect of supervising is collaboration, and to be a good collaborator you need to consistently and consciously exhibit civility. I have learned that Civility is a continuous

improvement strategy for building strong interpersonal relationships at work.

Chapter 9 – Put on Your Work Boots, and Make Sure Your Radio is Charged
Sometimes work is tough. Sometimes people are going to disappoint you, and **sometimes your work (and even your life) will suck. But you're going to have to figure out, no one is going to hold your hand.** Figure out what makes you feel confident and strong. Be an adult and do what you have to do to get you through the next day.

Chapter 10 – You are Exactly Where you Want to Be
It does not matter what people say. People say all kinds of things for all kinds of reasons and you can't put a lot of stock into words. However, **how a person acts, usually tells you what he/she really thinks**, what his/her values are, and who he/she is as a person. We each have the power to make choices and devise a life we are proud of, and where we are is a reflection of those choices.

Chapter 11 – Sources and Resources

About Christian Masotti

With over 25 years in the workforce, Christian understands that being civil and exhibiting "human-kindness" is a critical leadership competency that not only builds trust and credibility, but also impacts bottom line metrics including safety, quality, delivery, engagement, and efficiency. *"Many people perceive having respect, exhibiting kindness, and treating people well, as a sign of weakness – but this,* according to Civility Experts Inc. Director of Business Development Christian Masotti, *"is a costly mistake."*

A graduate of McGill University with years of field experience in OEM manufacturing environments including GM, Ford, and Chrysler, Christian has seen how when leaders have the courage to make decisions, give feedback, measure success based on quantitative observations, and to continually try to do all this in a civil way, they can create and/or change workplace culture.

Christian is a continuous learner who believes that the ability to combine his technical skills including Lean, Six Sigma and Kaizen with social intelligence and cultural competence has been the key to his success. In addition to consulting, keynote presentations, and delivery and design of training with Civility Experts Inc and its 501 affiliates in 48 countries, Christian's current projects include work with Maple Leaf Sports and Entertainment and Arcelor Mittal.

Social Competence for Manufacturing Supervisors is a Toolkit for anyone transitioning to a supervisory role in manufacturing. Christian is also the author of *Lean on Civility: Strategies for Changing Culture* in Manufacturing Workplaces, due for release March 2020.

Social Competence for Manufacturing Supervisors – Background

For a period of about 3 years, from late 2017 to presently, Christian worked multiple jobs concurrently. He was supervising conversions for Maple Leaf Sports and Entertainment, while working as a Supervisor at Bombardier and later Arcelor Mittal as a Production Supervisor, and at the same time consulting and training with Civility Experts Inc. as a Continuous Improvement Expert. At one point due to working all these jobs simultaneously, Christian had three phones and a radio. Thus, the reference to the subheading, *Three Phones and a Radio*.

The radio was a walkie-talkie and the phones were modern, but it seemed necessary to reference the fact that even with all the technology, Christian still had to rely on face-to-face, nonverbal, and verbal communication skills to do his job(s). This recognition – that at the end of the day it is old-fashioned, "high-touch" versus "high-tech" interaction that facilitates working well with others, was the impetus for the book.

Over 20+ years in manufacturing Christian has learned many lessons – and those related to the people side of supervising, relationships, building trust, the art of conversation, etc. The skills required to be successful as a supervisor had nothing to do with technology and in most cases, called on what some consider to be "old-fashioned" attitudes about how to treat people combined with tried and tested communication strategies.

Recognizing that this "people-treatment" component is what made all the difference between poor supervisors and great supervisors, and assessing that these specific skills are lacking in most new and/or young leaders, Christian decided to share some of the key lessons he had learned over the years.

Rationale and Supports for the Book

- In the *Leadership 2030 Report* by The Hay Group, researchers suggest that the time of a "post-heroic" leader is over. "The time of the alpha male — of the dominant, typically male leader who knows everything, who gives direction to everybody and sets the pace, whom everybody follows because this person is so smart and intelligent and clever — this time is over. We need a new kind of leader who focuses much more on relationships and understands that leadership is not about himself...this new leader is "altrocentric". It's the opposite of the egocentric leader. "Altrocentric" means focusing on others. Such a leader doesn't put himself at the very center. He knows he needs to listen to other people. He knows he needs to be intellectually curious and emotionally open. He knows that he needs empathy to do the job, not just in order to be a good person"[5].
- PeopleFirst Productivity Solutions, research suggests that there are 5 areas of supervisory skill that are critical for new supervisors[6] Listed below, you will note that 4 of the 5 skills relate directly to people-side of supervising.

    - People skills ("soft" skills)
    - Setting expectations, managing performance
    - Communication
    - People development

---

[5] https://www.washingtonpost.com/news/on-leadership/wp/2014/02/25/leadership-skills-for-the-year-2030/?noredirect=on

[6] https://blog.peoplefirstps.com/connect2lead/first-time-supervisors-success

- o   Technical skills

- Expanding on the Forbes article by Liz Ryan, 7 skill areas where most managers are deficit include[7]:
    - o   Perspective-taking
    - o   Allowing
    - o   Intellectual curiosity
    - o   Critical thinking
    - o   Connecting the dots
    - o   Humility
    - o   Coaching skills

- Consider the sample Production Supervisor Job Description[8] below. (Chapter 15)

---

[7] https://www.forbes.com/sites/lizryan/2016/05/26/seven-leadership-skills-most-managers-lack/#ed850867ebb3

[8] https://hiring.monster.com/employer-resources/job-description-templates/production-supervisor-job-description-sample/

About Lewena Bayer- Contributor

For more than 20 years, Lewena Bayer has led the Civility Experts Inc. team of almost 501 affiliates in 48 countries. As founder and CEO of the company, Lewena is recognized internationally as a leading expert on civility in the workplace. She is a 16-time published author, professional trainers, and in-demand speaker.

In addition to contributions to *Three Phones and a Radio*, Lewena Bayer and Christian Masotti have collaborated on an innovative training program and associated booked called *Manufacturing Civility*, and Christian's ground-breaking book *Lean on Civility* – used and referenced in several business and academic programs around the world. Christian supports the Civility Experts Global team as a Business Development Consultant, facilitator, speaker, and continuous improvement advisor. Christian is also a contributor to Dr. Bayer's new book, *Civility at Work*.

Lessons and Social Competence Strategies Summary Chart

LESSON	STRATEGY	SKILLS	APPLICATION
Don't be quick to judge, people will surprise you. **Touches on:** -Why supervisors lack restraint -Off standard conditions - scenarios where the Examples of bias -Two wait for it strategy applies -Brain-restraint -The 24- rule hour -Nonjudgment	Wait for it	Restraint Non-judgment	Enables fair assessment of others, decreases reactive thinking, and helps remove bias.
People want to feel valued, trusted, and respected **Touches on:** -Typical manufacturing culture -What "rough" means -People treatment -Persona -Being nice -Reasons not to be nice -Benefits of being nice	Be nice	Civility	Builds trust, helps establish personal credibility and promotes fair and good people treatment
Technology and paperwork cannot replace face-to-face interaction	Get out there and talk to people	Get out there and talk to people	Builds trust, fosters rapport and positive regard and

with people. **Touches** on: -Reasons why supervisors avoid people -Social Intelligence -Organizational culture -Presence -Elements of Social Competence -SPACE theory			supports effective communication.
You have to be willing to learn, ongoing, and from others. **Touches on:** -People resources -Continuous learning -Habits of continuous learners -Tribal knowledge -Reasons we ignore people resources -Mentors -Continuous learning tools	Apply continuous learning to connect with people	Continuous Learning	Enables you to benefit from a mentor and to access tribal knowledge. Facilitates individual ability to adapt to change.
Consistent character will often outperform supervisors who are smarter or work harder. **Touches on:** -Lying -Character -Types of Honesty -Signs of prolific lying	Always tell the truth	Honesty	Build credibility, supports trust-building.

26

-HEXACO Model -Social cues that indicate lying -Building trust			
If you are paying attention, people will almost always tell you what they really want. **Touches on:** -Building rapport -Listening -Attention span -Barriers to communication -End in mind listening -Types of purpose -Types of questions -Listening with TING	Ask questions	Ask strategic and timely questions	Enables you to build rapport and trust while not being too personal. Helps you acquire information and supports you need.
You are going to get knocked down, you have to learn to take a punch. **Touches on:** -Proverbial punch -Resilience -Indicators of resilience -Mental exhaustion -Benefits of resilience -8 ways to build mental fortitude	Learn to bounce back from psychological punches	Resilience	Enables you to manage ongoing psychological and emotional stress. Overcome barriers to success, build trusting relationships.
Collaboration is currency in the new world of work. **Touches on:** -Leveraging skills	Foster collaboration	Collaboration	Enables you to acquire information quickly and achieve results by leveraging and

-Collaboration versus teamwork -Civility -How to teach collaboration -How to create workplace culture to foster collaboration			sharing skills. Fosters shared values.
Work and life can be tough, but no one will hold your hand. Figure out what you need to do to be strong and get through. **Touches on:** -Hard work -Hardiness -The 40 percent Rule -3 Aspects of Hardiness -Indicators of Hardiness -3 Cs of Hardiness -Managing long work days -Benefits of hardiness	Be a strong competitor	Hardiness: -Physicality -Confidence -Self-direction	Enables you to survive and even thrive in stressful settings. Helps you feel empowered and in control. Builds self-respect and autonomy.
People say all kinds of things, but what they do shows you who they really are. **Touches on:** -Talking versus doing -Happy at work -The Peter Principle -Responsibility -Accountability -How to teach responsibility	Be responsible	Personal Responsibility	Fosters maturity and respect of others Builds trust and helps you achieve a quality life and career.

Chapter 1
Wait for it!

> *"When you go into a situation with an open mind and you assume the best of people, when you accept them on the surface without judgment, people can surprise you, and it is equally surprising how much you can learn, about yourself, and about others, when you wait for it.* – Christian Masotti

Sometimes the "ah-ha" happens almost immediately, and sometimes truly seeing (not just looking at) what is right in front of you, can take days, or weeks, or years. Sadly, some people never see what is right in front of them. Based on my experience, in the case of supervisors (new or experienced) this happens for one of three reasons:

a) Sometimes people simply don't care enough about something to pay attention.
b) Sometimes people just don't have the awareness or ability to recognize or interpret what they see or experience beyond a general physical interpretation.
c) Sometimes people are too quick to assess what they are experiencing, e.g., due to immaturity, ego, fear, ignorance, or other factors, and so they miss the most important aspects or the deeper meaning.

Over the years, I have come to understand that it is important to slow down and take time to not only observe but also to take time to interpret what you observe. This can be difficult to do even when you know it's important, especially for supervisors who frequently find themselves in time-strained, unexpected, and stressful situations where it may be perceived that quick thinking is required.

In my experience, there are at least two scenarios where supervisors MUST learn to apply the "wait for it" strategy. The first is when things seem easy to interpret or obvious.

Sometimes things are not as simple as they appear and if you don't observe with an open mind, your assumptions and bias can skew your interpretations of things. It's human nature to fall back on our experiences and to apply what we think we know for sure. However, in manufacturing environments, there are so many factors influencing a situation at any given time, and things change so quickly, that what you thought you knew for sure e.g., yesterday, a week ago, or even an hour ago, is frequently no longer accurate or relevant.

Some examples of bias might include:

- Judgements about age, gender, education, or culture
- Perceptions about rank, status, and privilege
- Expectations about what represents "respect"
- Experiences from the past, e.g., how your previous boss behaved
- Opinions of others, e.g., someone you know on the job or someone you trust
- Routines or habits that you may or may not be aware of, e.g., you always told jokes before and it went over well, so why not now?
- Pieces of information from popular culture or what you perceive to be an expert source

The second scenario where the "wait for it" strategy is helpful, occurs when people, circumstances, or events seem to make no sense. I call this "off standard". Rather than rush to concluding that the situation is complex or immediately assuming you can't handle it, and so escalating the issue or getting others involved, I have learned that if you should just pause. Watch and wait a bit. With a little time, almost all the answers you need will become apparent to you and/or sooner than you think, the situation resolves itself. Naturally, we are not talking about high-risk safety or safety or compliance situations here. Clearly, in those cases, immediate action should be taken according to protocol and prescribed processes.

When I suggest that things often resolve themselves, what I mean is:
- Sometimes the person(s) responsible for the off standard activity or event recognize their role and take steps to resolve things themselves
- Sometimes there are extenuating conditions that pass, and the situation resolves itself
- Sometimes a helpful co-worker or team member realizes the issue and fixes whatever it is.

While supervisors should always be paying attention and observing any off standard situation, what I'm saying is that they don't always need to rush in to take action and save the day.

The ability to "wait for it" turns out to be a skill that many people never acquire. But it's worth learning because when you have restraint and patience enough to wait for people and things to reveal themselves to you, all kinds of good things happen.

For example, when you wait for it you are more likely to:

- Realize the value of an experience
- Find clarity on complex issues
- Recognize the character and/or contributions of others
- Become aware of conscious and unconscious bias
- Understand the benefits, costs, or consequences of a decision
- Be perceived as credible
- Begin to see connections between people, processes, and systems
- Draw on the expertise, knowledge, and experience of others

The ability to restrain oneself is an aspect of experiential knowledge that I now understand to be wisdom. Looking back over my life and experiences I can see where, and how, being patient, taking time to make decisions, and/or just waiting for situations and relationships to unfold, has served me well.

One way I apply this strategy on the job is to avoid soliciting or indulging the opinions of others. Specifically, I avoid their opinions about other team members. This is good advice for new supervisors. When you are a new supervisor, new to an environment, maybe a bit nervous about what you know or don't know, and of course wanting to fit in, it is tempting to pay too much attention to all the people who seem more than happy to give you information. There are always "good guys" who immediately approach you, seem to want to help you find your way around, and are overall seeming eager to help. Be careful. When you are stressed or vulnerable, it is easy to take in this freely-offered insight and advice – and some of it may be honest, good, or useful – but, it is dangerous to accept everything you hear as fact. You must remember that subconsciously (due to your vulnerability when you are new) you may be giving more weight to this information than you realize.

It has been my practice not to engage in these types of communications or to solicit the opinion of others until I have had a chance to do my own tour, review of process/data, observe people on the job, conduct some research, etc. This enables me to form my own opinion of someone rather than let my experience with that person be influenced (positively or negatively) by the information or impression of others.
More than once, I've been told, "Watch out for Bob, he is lazy", or "Pete's a good guy", "Janet is the nicest person you'll ever meet", "If you want to know about x, do not ask John, he knows nothing", etc. If I then go into interactions with these people whom I've never met and already have an idea who they are or what they know etc., there is a pretty good chance that whatever they do or say will be interpreted in a way that supports the viewpoints that were shared with me. The encounter then potentially becomes a self-fulfilling prophecy that doesn't benefit anyone.

Another example of what the "wait for it" strategy looks like in practice is "The 24-hour rule." I use this rule in both my professional and personal life and find it to be an effective tool. Many sports organizations use this rule as a way of managing tensions between parents and coaches, but the strategy also works well in workplaces.

The 24-hour rule has several purposes:

1) Allows each party involved during an issue to step back and clear the initial emotional elements
2) Provides a clear and concise process for problem resolution
3) Provides a clear understanding of what is expected from all parties involved
4) Promotes direct communication
5) Provides an avenue of fairness and opportunity to every parent, player, and coach

Sample Description of The 24-Hour Rule

> When an issue occurs and a party has a resulting complaint to make or issue to be resolved, they are asked to wait 24 hours, then put the issue in writing and submit it to the appropriate party. Whether this issue is labelled as coaching error, teammate interference, parent conflict or any other of a number of possible situations, it is very important that all parties involved take the full 24 hours to remove or decrease the emotional element so that the actual issue can be resolved quickly, in a civilized manner, and to everyone's satisfaction.
>
> We at Wallace Minor Hockey realize that from time to time, an issue may occur, which is why the time was taken to develop this policy and provide that avenue to all of our members.
>
> Wallace Minor Hockey prides itself on its family-

like atmosphere and its ability to communicate directly with all members by not losing sight of what is most important - all players having fun playing hockey[9].

The 24-hour rule is an example of changing behaviour through policy or process versus trying to change an attitude or belief. This can be a very effective strategy when supervising people. Rules, codes of conduct, guidelines, regulations all serve to obligate people to behave a certain way regardless of whether they agree with the behaviour or not.

How often, whether in your personal or professional life, have you been reminded not to judge a book by its cover? The human tendency to jump to quick conclusions, e.g., about overall competence, confidence, education, and/or personality, among other qualities, has become a comprehensive field of study. The science of snap judgments is more than just figuring out what we can tell by looking at each other. Knowing how people size each other up from day to day has significant implications for identifying and subduing implicit bias, discrimination, and stereotyping. Furthermore, research[10] by Nicholas Rule an assistant professor in the department of psychology at the University of Toronto, Canada, shows that even in cases where we already have a lot of information, a snap judgment overpowers decision making.

The fact is, some of us have highly tuned social radar such that we have the ability to read verbal, nonverbal, tonal and contextual cues accurately. However, in this age of distraction, many of us do not have this skill. When you add low social radar to situations where a diverse work team may exhibit different or unfamiliar cues, and where conditions are noisy, often dangerous or stressful, it is easy to make quick but

---

[9] https://wallacesabres.com/Pages/1109/What_To_Do_-_The_24-Hour_Rule/

[10] https://www.psychologicalscience.org/observer/snap-judgment-science

incorrect judgments. In addition, for younger generations who have grown up relying on Google or social media circles for facts and opinions, intuition may not be honed sufficient to be reliable.

The science suggests that our perceptions are so conditioned to being influenced by our subconscious, that we don't even realize when bias, past experience, memory, or emotion are potentially clouding our judgment.

In workplace settings, particularly if you are in a leadership role, first impressions can have a significant impact on how relationships develop and this can have a further impact on productivity, performance assessments, perceptions of promote-ability, etc. This shouldn't be surprising. Consider for example that literature suggests there are valid facial cues that assist us in assessing someone's health or intelligence, but such cues are overshadowed by an 'attractiveness halo' whereby desirable attributions are preferentially ascribed to attractive people. The impact of the attractiveness halo effect on perceptions of academic performance in the classroom is concerning as this has shown to influence students' future performance[11].

By teaching oneself to "wait for it", you are in a way applying a personal code of conduct – that is, requiring yourself to behave in a way that facilitates restraint and offsets the potentially negative impact of quick judgment.

Key Take-Away:

If you go into interactions and communications with an open-mind and deliberately practice non-judgment, people will often surprise you. If you wait for people to reveal themselves to you, it is astonishing what you can learn about them.

---

[11] https://journals.plos.org/plosone/article?id=10.1371/journal.pone.0148284

Social Competence Skill Supervisors Need: Non-Judgment via Restraint

In order to be able to apply the "wait for it" strategy, you need to be able to have the following skills:

- Restraint- A physical halt which includes a verbal ability to pause, to be quiet, to hold still, to take no action for a measured amount of time, and to be calm, and neutral while you wait
- Brain-restraint (A Masotti term) Psychological restraint, which means suspending judgment and avoiding jumping to conclusions. Of course, your general brain activity doesn't stop, the idea is that you deliberately stall aspects of your thinking patterns or habits. For just a few minutes, don't think. Experience and observe without judgment

The ability to exercise physical restraint comes with deliberate practice, and with maturity. Often an inability to restrain oneself physically is due to a weak ego, e.g., having to be center of attention, needing to be right or wanting to show power over someone else, and some of this is offset just by growing up. We learn as we experience various consequences that patience is indeed a valuable virtue. Low ability to restrain can also be due to low emotional intelligence (lack of self-awareness) and/or low social intelligence (inability to read social cues and act appropriately in various social settings).

The ability to exercise brain-restraint requires acknowledging that we all harbor various biases. Brain restraint requires consciously suspending the influence that our past experiences, our fears, our expectations, etc., have over how we make snap judgments about people, places, conditions, and events. This ability to suspend judgment, even when one is willing and wanting to make the effort, is not easy.

Psychologists once believed that only bigoted people raced to judgment and used stereotypes. Now the study of unconscious bias is revealing the unsettling truth: we all use stereotypes, all the time, without knowing it. We have met the enemy of equality, and the enemy is us. In the early 1980s, theories about stereotypes were concerned only with their explicit expression: outright and unabashed racism, sexism, anti-Semitism. But in the years since, a new approach to stereotypes has shattered that simple notion. Unconscious bias is something far more subtle, and more insidious: what's known as automatic or implicit stereotyping, which, research shows, we do all the time without knowing it. How progressive a person seems to be on the surface bears little or no relation to how prejudiced he or she is on an unconscious level.[12]

Over years of work in the field, the research team at Civility Experts Inc., has come to understand that the ability to exercise non-judgment underpins the ability to be civil. This is because you cannot convey respect (which is a key aspect of civility) if you do not truly believe each person is of equal value. However, if you perceive each individual as having equal value, you do not concern yourself with measuring the person at the time of first impression. Rather you see the person as a human being first. You work to acknowledge the person, make him/her comfortable, and then keep an open mind and strive to make fact-based assessments of knowledge, skill, and ability pertinent to the job. When you acknowledge that others have something to contribute- even when you don't know what that is, and when you show acceptance and respect for a person, even when you don't understand or know him or her, you are exhibiting civility. That we automatically respect each other regardless of age, race, gender, education etc., is critical to building a workplace culture of civility.

I agree with Civility Experts Inc. assertion that respect is

---

[12] https://www.psychologytoday.com/ca/articles/199805/where-bias-begins-the-truth-about-stereotypes

something that people are entitled to, just because they are human and on the planet. This idea is an ongoing debate outside of civility practitioner circles. Many people refer to civility as something you have to earn or something that others have to prove. This is in fact, contrary to civility. But that people are NOT equal, e.g. union versus management, man versus woman, production worker versus supervisor, college/university educated versus trade-skilled, and the disrespect and judgment that these labels create is ingrained in most manufacturing cultures.

> "If you are a civil person, you may not always trust people, you may not always like them, or understand them, but you do have to respect them. To respect them, you must acknowledge that they have the same rights and privileges to belief systems to personal values, to choices and preferences and decisions, as you do. You must be able to accept that each human being is of equal value on a basic human level and acknowledge that each of us has a gift or something to offer. The gift (in the workplace the gift relates to a skill or competency) may be known or unknown, and it may go unrecognized or unused, but none of us has the right to assess that gift or the human being who has it, in a way that reduces that person's value. It is very difficult to accept another human being as equal in value, and then to concurrently judge that person. This is an important recognition for anyone in leadership positions. Of course, you must assess and judge behaviour, but this is different from judging a person"[13].

How Do You Teach Non-Judgment?

It is important for adults who are judgmental to be made aware that judgments are simply statements (conscious or unconscious/verbal or nonverbal), they are not facts. Once people are aware of when and how they are being judgmental,

---

[13] Dr. Lewena Bayer, CEO Civility Experts Inc.

they can then be encouraged to ask themselves where the judgment comes from.

What is the statement of judgment grounded in? Often people don't even know where the idea they have in their head or are communicating outwardly (which usually reflects a bias or stereotype) came from. Supervisors must learn, and be able to teach others, that if there is no factual basis for a statement, that statement/judgment cannot be considered valid. It is simply an opinion. An effective supervisor's view should always require that information is quantifiable.

In manufacturing environments, some common judgments/bias include:

- Perceptions about unions
- Assumptions about management priorities
- Beliefs about appropriateness or abilities of women on the job
- Expectations about "grandfathered" rights and privileges of long-term employees
- Expectations about heritage jobs, e.g., positions passed on to family
- Attitudes about value of on the job experience over education
- Attitudes about change

One strategy for teaching the restraint that supports non-judgment is to encourage people to pause before they speak or take any action. That they pause is important, and once they agree with this, the next step is to teach when and how long to pause. How long they pause might relate to factors such as:

- Overall risk
- Level of emotion
- Relationship between the parties involved
- Physical conditions, e.g., am I tired, stressed, hungry
- Workplace role and responsibility

- Personal biases or blind spots

Teaching restraint doesn't necessarily have to be a formal training endeavor. People can learn the "wait for it" strategy by observing those they respect or follow exhibiting it. And/or you can encourage the behaviour, e.g., implement a 24-hour policy for interpersonal issues, and trust that the attitude and mindset shift will follow – it usually does once people begin to experience the positive feedback and improvement in their relationships as a result of applying the strategy. A behaviour checklist below.

Masotti Commonsense Social Competence Strategy #1: Wait for It.

- ☐ Pause deliberately to assess the situation
- ☐ Resist saying anything immediately
- ☐ Suspend your thoughts, e.g., don't make assumptions, don't jump to conclusions, set aside any bias or expectations
- ☐ Listen to the other person
- ☐ Pay attention to the context, e.g., what is going on around you?
- ☐ Watch the other person's nonverbal cues Ask questions using a calm, polite tone
- ☐ Avoid starting your sentences with "I" in an effort to be other-focused
- ☐ Be self-aware. Pay attention to when you make snap judgments and work to understand why you have jumped to conclusions and then set those judgments aside.

  Non-judgment requires self-awareness. You must examine your own biases, both conscious and unconscious, and go into every interaction, assuming the best of people -Lew Bayer, CEO Civility Experts Inc.

Please see Chapter 11 for Sources and Resources for ongoing learning.

Chapter 2
Just Be Nice!

In real life at work, most people just want to feel valued, trusted, and respected. If you can achieve this and be perceived as a decent human being – most other attributes account for very little. - Christian Masotti

I would not describe the typical manufacturing plant as a nice place to work. While some of the people might be nice some of the time, the workplace itself is not very nice. Manufacturing can be dirty work under harsh conditions, tight timelines, constant change, and ever-increasing demands to do more with less. As a result, the overall tone of the environment is far from nice.

Maybe it's because manufacturing has traditionally been male-dominated, or because the work is perceived to be strenuous or physical and the conditions tough, that the tendency has been for leadership to be "rough" on their teams. By rough I mean, stereotypically "male". No weak behaviour tolerated. No crying, no touchie-feelie nonsense, and no acting like you care about anything other than getting the job done. Basically no "nice" is expected or allowed. Nice is for the weak.

In traditional manufacturing environments, you need to show you are not weak. Fitting in often requires being "rough" which might include engaging in behaviours such as:

- Swearing
- Calling people names
- Ignoring people
- Criticizing people in public
- Walking away when people are talking to you
- Shouting
- Demonstrating physical strength, e.g., punching a wall,

- stomping, making a fist
- Toughing it out when you experience small injuries
- Crowding others, e.g., getting into their personal space
- Overtalking and/or interrupting
- Rolling your eyes
- Gesturing rudely e.g., giving the finger
- Shutting people down verbally
- Speaking in a harsh tone
- Taking a staunch stance, e.g., wide postures
- Failing to acknowledge others
- Avoiding showing softness, e.g., formal thank you, hugging, too much smiling
- Avoiding apologizing

And generally, just not being nice.

As a result of this "be strong to survive" mindset, manufacturing plants are not perceived as great places to work. Sure the noise, the time constraints, the stress, the union aspects, etc. all contribute to a what can be described as a toxic workplace culture, but mostly, the lack of niceness is due to leadership (including supervisors and managers) and their respective attitudes toward what constitutes acceptable "people treatment". People treatment is a civility term that refers to an overall attitude about what constitutes a fair and good way of interacting with people. It includes how you speak, nonverbal gestures, the extent to which you are empathetic, and how you define honesty and integrity.

When I trained to be a Master Civility Trainer, one of the key messages I took away is that civility is a choice. Most of us know what is right and wrong, but with regard to people treatment,

> "[…] good people sometimes make bad decisions about how to treat others due in large part to relinquishing their personal power to others, or due to perceived

expectations or pressure in specific environments."[14]

This suggests that people treatment is a complex dynamic, but basically nurture – workplace culture in this case, rather than nature- the personal traits and qualities of the individuals in the culture, defines decision-making, especially related to interpersonal relationships and people-treatment. I believe this may be true of many manufacturing environments, and it was in fact true of several organizations where I worked.

Unfortunately, many people who work in the industry for a while find themselves taking on a "no more Mr. Nice Guy" persona when on the job. The environment almost demands it. I understand a "persona" to be the qualities and characteristics that you create or build in an effort to fit into a particular situation or role.

So, what does it mean to be "nice"? The word has mixed connotations. Who hasn't learned the hard way that "you're so nice" is a polite rejection? The word "nice" is generally defined as a constellation of traits that prioritize kindness, conscientiousness, warmth, and respect—but when it comes to romantic interest, NICE can be a shorthand antonym for bold, strong, or sexy, instead meaning "needy, weak, predictable, boring, inexperienced, and unattractive"[15].

For the purposes of our discussion in this chapter, being nice in a manufacturing environment doesn't mean being warm and fuzzy, or overtly kind or polite, it just means being courteous and decent. I would encourage all supervisors to incorporate aspects of being nice into their workplace persona, for example, at the very least you would:

- Acknowledge others, e.g., eye contact, saying hello, maybe a smile

---

[14] Lew Bayer, CEO of Civility Experts Inc

[15] Herold & Milhausen, 1999

- Consider the experience of others, e.g., if you're hungry, maybe they're hungry too
- Resist going out of your way to humiliate or embarrass people
- Exercise some restraint; don't yell or swear just because you can
- Say something positive now and then

On the surface adding a little bit of nice into the workplace doesn't seem like too much to ask, but clearly, it's not easy to change hundreds of years of tradition in manufacturing culture. Consider for example, that in many ways, society supports the old-school manufacturing notion that it doesn't pay to be nice, a few reasons here:

Don't be nice, reason A. Being too nice at work can impact your reputation. According to Business Media[16] being too nice can result in people:

- Perceiving you as boring
- Deciding not to listen to you e.g., if they prefer drama
- Taking advantage of you, e.g., sometimes nice people say can't say "no"
- Having higher expectations of you, e.g., expect you to help out more
- Being suspicious of you e.g., not believe that you are authentically as nice as you are
- Failing to value you
- Determining that you are not equal to them
- Seeing you as weak
- Overlooking you, e.g., sometimes nice people don't get noticed due to less drama and attention-seeking behaviour

---

[16] https://www.businessinsider.com/being-too-nice-at-work-can-backfire-2014-9

Don't be nice, reason B. Being nice can impact your health. For the most part, I was able to be successful in my supervisory positions without being too much of an ass!%!*, (most of the time anyway) and while there were some positive long-term benefits to making this effort, there is no question that the stress of doing so impacted my health in some ways, at various points in my career.

Research published in *Psychology Today* suggests that in fact, working too hard to be nice, can take a toll[17], for example, personal health consequences may include:

- Internalization resulting in addictions, depression, and anxiety
- Periodic acting out when the stress gets to be too much
- Self-criticism – blaming yourself and taking on other people's responsibilities and problems
- Resentment when it becomes obvious that you are not appreciated or that others are taking advantage or getting ahead without being nice
- Burnout because you are so busy taking care of others that you forget to take care of yourself
- Pre-compromising in relationships, for example, you might downgrade your personal wants and needs in lieu of what you anticipate others might want or need
- Appearing controlling or passive at times for example when you are either too tired to care or care too much
- Later life regrets when you potentially feel like everyone else was taking care of him/herself and you missed out on your own life because you were not self-focused
- Stale relationships because in being nice you are maybe not always honest about how you feel resulting in surface connections versus meaningful connections

---

[17] https://www.psychologytoday.com/ca/blog/fixing-families/201807/the-dangers-being-nice

Don't be nice, reason C. Niceness can impact thinking skills. Not that this justifies uncivil workplace culture but believe it or not, *Quartz at Work* suggests that due to a phenomenon called "shared information bias" that happens in nice-focused workplaces, being nice can actually inhibit thinking skills. "Shared information bias[18]" refers to how individuals in a nice workplace learn that one of the best ways of making a group feel good and making their teammates see then as competent is to repeat and repackage information that everyone already knows. It makes the person sharing look smart and in-step with his/her colleagues even if he/she is just rehashing the same thing that was said last week or by a person who spoke a moment prior. As the heads start nodding and the good feeling starts spreading, critical thinking starts shutting down. Team members who hold contrary or novel information even begin to experience a type of amnesia as the pull of agreeableness focuses their attention on what the group already knows and erases potentially unique contributions from their memory banks. At the end of one of these nice-fests, everyone reports feeling happy, even the person whose perspective was silenced without quite realizing it.

Don't be nice, reason D. Nice guys often finish last. Sadly, it is true that in many organizations, not just manufacturing, that it is people who are not nice that get promoted. Sometimes, despite being terrible human beings, people get moved up the ladder just because they are in the right place at the right time. Sometimes, they're perceived to deserve a new role due to longevity, and regardless of competence or an ability to work well with others. Sometimes it's because their uncle owns the company, and sometimes they just sneak through. Regardless, many who find themselves in positions that they know they aren't capable of handling, live in a constant state of fearfulness. They are afraid their incompetence will be uncovered. They are afraid someone will challenge them or do a better job than them. And sometimes

---

[18] https://qz.com/work/1260571/at-work-a-respectful-culture-is-better-than-a-nice-one/

they are afraid of what would come next, e.g., although unqualified, the job they have is the only job they know, so they must fake it or figure it out because they have nowhere else to go. They are motivated by fear, and so they use fear as a strategy to motivate others. This is not nice.

Fearful people need to have other fearful people around them. They need to surround themselves with people who won't ask too many questions. They need people around them who will keep quiet and keep their heads down because they too are afraid of losing their jobs. They need people who will cover for them, and suck up to them and never let on that they know their higher up has no business being there. In these situations, ego and power playing overrides business success but surprisingly the work gets done.

I have learned that in these settings, toxic, under qualified managers and supervisors actually like chaos. They sometimes even create problems just to be perceived as heroes when they solve them. This is not nice. It's important to be civil and this is an effective social competence strategy that can help supervisors succeed.

As mentioned earlier in the chapter, as I experienced more and matured, I learned to be a successful supervisor AND be nice. I have made it my personal standard to consistently try to treat people as they would like to be treated. I don't yell just because someone else is yelling. I might swear about something, but rarely. And, I make it a personal rule never to swear *at* a person. I acknowledge people and say hello, even if they don't say hello back. I try to make eye contact. I try not to interrupt. I do my best to practice common courtesy, e.g., be on time, be prepared, listen more than I speak, give the benefit of the doubt, and I try to assume the best of people. As a result, I have frequently scored higher than my colleagues/peers on a range of metrics including:

- Exceeding production goals
- Building cooperative teams

- Meeting safety targets easily
- Implementing improvements via cooperative teams
- Retaining team members
- Adapting to change

In several workplaces, I have been able to achieve more or better than my not so nice counterparts simply by being civil. Sure, it's easier to be a jerk, but why not be different. Why not treat people like human beings? You might be surprised what an impact even the smallest civil gestures can have.

Statistics show that more than 80 percent of people are dissatisfied with their jobs[19]. This surprisingly has very little to do with compensation. The reality is people are stressed out and this is largely due to being treated badly by their colleagues and higher-ups.

It pays to be polite and follow general social rules, e.g., exhibit common courtesy. But "nice" is more about how you make people feel than about following social rules. It's about making an effort to show people that they have value, that you see them as people first, and people doing a job second. There is tremendous power in being nice. In addition to the human capital and relational wealth benefits, there is potential for increased profitability too.

A growing body of research supports the idea that civility can have a positive impact to bottom line business metrics:
- According to the American Psychological Association, when employees feel valued by their employer, 92 percent say they are satisfied with their job, 91 percent say they are motivated to do their best, and 89 percent are more likely to report being in good psychological health[20]

---

[19] http://www.businessinsider.com/disturbing-facts-about-your-job-2011-2?op=1#ixzz3XCZH6nbq

[20] http://www.apaexcellence.org/assets/general/2015-phwa-oea-magazine.pdf

- Companies that openly promote civil communication among employees earn 30 percent more revenue than competitors, are four times more likely to have highly engaged employees and are 20 percent more likely to report reduced turnover.[21]
- In a Civility, Respect, and Engagement in the Workplace (CREW) intervention, a six-month process that fosters civil interactions between employees. Participants in the intervention experienced increases in civility with decreases in workplace distress and incivility after completing CREW. These improvements continued to increase one year after the intervention ended[22]

Key Take-Away

It does not matter whether you are old, young, male, female, charismatic, good looking, rich, poor, overweight, smoke, don't smoke, are experienced, are inexperienced, are a person of culture, or somehow different than the people you work with, at the end of the day, people will remember how you make them feel. In real life at work, most people want to feel valued, trusted and respected. You can achieve this in large part, by just being nice.

Social Competence Skill Supervisors Need: Civility

To be effective at building solid working relationships, supervisors need to learn that being "nice" means that at the very least you follow social rules for common courtesy. This is one aspect of choosing civility. Beyond this general approach,

---

[21] Watson Wyatt Civility Survey, http://www.towerswatson.com/

[22] Leiter, M. P., Day, A., Oore, D. G., & Laschinger, H. K. S. (2012). Getting better and staying better: Assessing civility, incivility, distress, and job attitudes one year after a civility intervention. *Journal of Occupational Health Psychology, 17*(4), 425-434.

you choose to do more than the basics in terms of common courtesy and choose to do what is perceived as the good and right thing in a certain social situation. Often the "good and right thing" from an interpersonal relationship perspective is choosing the action that will somehow ease the experience of the other person. There is no question that etiquette rules and social guidelines (some of which includes workplace policy and codes of conduct) help us to make decisions about what is expected and respected behaviour in various settings. However, simply following the rules because you are supposed to, doesn't make you a nice person, or a good person, or a civil person. It just makes you a person who follows the rules.

Choosing to exhibit civility means that you are consciously aware of the impact your words and actions have. It means that you make deliberate choices to treat people in a way that eases their experience. Civility means thinking about how an individual might need or want to be treated versus assuming that everyone wants to be treated the same way. From an interpersonal point of view, civility means treating people in a way that shows them that you value and respect them. This treatment can look very different in different settings. For example, following a social rule, e.g., extending a handshake, can potentially cause discomfort to someone of a different culture, even though your intention was to show respect by following a social protocol.

Civility requires paying attention. And in workplace settings, being "nice" as part of being civil requires that you constantly weigh accountability as well as feelings. For example, you have an obligation to be honest, ethical, transparent, and in many cases to address the priorities of the workplace.

This means that in some cases, being "nice" might require giving constructive criticism or engaging in difficult conversations. *How* you give feedback and/or how you approach difficult conversations is where civility comes in.

How Do You Teach Civility?

On the surface it may seem like exhibiting civility is easy. Being nice *should* be easy, however, many people struggle with even basic common courtesy. But exhibiting civility can be more difficult. Choosing civility can be difficult because making the choice to consistently treat people in a fair and good way requires a mindset shift including:

- Changing our typical view that respect is something people need to earn, to understanding that respect is something we are all deserving of just because we are human beings
- Recognizing that respect should be given with no expectation of return, that is, you recognize value in people and treat them well regardless of whether doing so benefits you directly or not
- Understanding that there is a cost to being civil; it takes time, thoughtfulness, energy, and sometimes personal resources
- Being able to differentiate between respectful people treatment (valuing others) and trust building behaviour
- Anticipating that where civility is not typically exhibited, people don't always respond to it the way you think they will, e.g., they don't believe you mean to be kind just to be kind, they fear they will be expected to change to be civil too, they simply don't like change, etc.

Civility is:
- A conscious awareness of the impact of one's thoughts, actions, words and intentions on others; combined with,

- A continuous acknowledgement of one's responsibility to ease the experience of others (e.g., through restraint, kindness, non-judgment, respect, and courtesy); and,

- A consistent effort to adopt and exhibit civil behaviour as a non-negotiable point of one's character.[23]

Civility is not just about having manners or being kind. Civility is a measurable competency. There are at least four core skills that we need to learn to be able to be civil. These skills are:
- Social Intelligence
- Cultural Competence
- Systems Thinking
- Continuous Learning

You can teach each of the four core skills related to ability to be civil, and this is time well spent. Doing so is surprisingly cost-effective and certainly worth the investment, but for the most part, you learn to be civil by experiencing it. For this reason, supervisors need to learn to be civil so that they can lead by example. This is why I recommend training supervisors and managers in civility competencies versus training the whole front line.

Experts in the field suggest that because uncivil behaviour is often grounded in mindset, or fear, or bias, you must change the behaviour and hope that the shift in attitude follows. For example, if someone is yelled at constantly by a manager, and so performs so as not to be yelled at, he/she might adopt yelling as his/her own communication style. If this person doesn't see that he/she can achieve the same results without yelling, he/she won't see the benefits and so has no incentive to change behaviour. As a result, the uncivil cycle continues. Most adults need to experience something different and beneficial before they will change their behaviour.

Aspects of some of these civility-focused skills are covered in this book, but it is well worth your time to seek resources and training in these competency areas. Generally, if you have limited time and resources, but you want to engage in formal

---

[23] Lew Bayer

training, the suggestion would be to begin with Social Intelligence. Social intelligence refers to your ability to read verbal, nonverbal, tonal, and contextual cues effectively and in a timely way. This skill is easy to learn and applying it has an almost immediate positive impact. Additional information about Social Intelligence is covered in Chapter 3.

Masotti Commonsense Social Competence Strategy #2: Just Be Nice

- Pause, wait…take a breath, compose yourself, think about what you will say or do BEFORE you do it
- Assume the best of others; try to set aside any personal issues, history with the individual, personal needs, known biases, etc
- Consider social protocol. What do the social rules (written or unwritten) suggest is the appropriate response or behaviour in this setting and/or situation?
- Think about what you want to happen next, e.g., how do you want to be perceived, how do you want the other person to feel, what do you want the outcome of the interaction/communication to be?
- Consider the time and place, e.g., is this the right time for the communication? Should you go somewhere private? Do you need a 3rd party to witness? Does the other party need time to compose him/herself?
- Be kind;
    - Choose words and/or actions that show you at your best and do not cause harm to the other person
    - Make eye contact as a way of acknowledging others
    - Extend general greetings, e.g., say hello
    - Maintain a calm and moderate tone, e.g., don't yell
    - Avoid swearing

- ☐ Close with a verbal or physical handshake, e.g., shake hands, say thank you for X, look the person in the eye. OR, acknowledge and close the interaction verbally, e.g., say, "So, we are all good then?", or "See you tomorrow then" or something to show you anticipate a positive and future interaction.

"The most important single ingredient in the formula of success is knowing how to get along with people." - Theodore Roosevelt

Please see Chapter 11 for Sources and Resources for ongoing learning.

Chapter 3
Don't Be the Donut and Clipboard Guy

"At some point, you're going to have to engage with people. Technology and paperwork cannot replace the power of face-to-face interaction". – Christian Masotti

"Busy" is not the same thing as "productive". Many times, I've worked with people who are constantly doing something; rushing around, sweating, sighing heavily, keeping busy…pretending they know what they're doing, but not getting anything done. They look busy, but they are not productive.

Just as often I've worked with leaders who spend the majority of their shifts behind a desk or hiding out in their offices. Occasionally they come down to the floor, clipboard in hand. Typically, these rare visits to the production floor are an effort to reach out to the team members that they haven't interacted with for far too long. These clipboard wielding guys/gals usually offer up treats- pizza, donuts, tickets to one thing or another, etc.

Sure, the treats are appreciated. I mean who doesn't like pizza, right? But these supervisors are not fooling anyone and contrary to what they might think, these types of gestures are not credibility builders. Quite the opposite in fact. Believe me, you do not want to be the supervisor who everyone knows as the "donut guy" – the supervisor they never see except on Friday when he/she is doing the two-minute manager routine. In my experience supervisors who use a clipboard as a social shield, hide out in their office, or try to cover up incompetence by currying favor with food, do so for one of the following reasons:
   a) They are in way over their head and don't really understand what their job is, e.g., maybe they think the paperwork is the priority.

b) They are on some level scared of the people on the production floor.
c) They know what they need to do in terms of the people-side of the work, but they don't have the skills to do it.

If the reason a supervisor isn't interacting with the people on the floor is in fact because of a) above, that is, he/she doesn't know that doing so is a key function of the role, there sometimes isn't too much you can do about this. In many manufacturing environments, the job still gets done. If management is solely focused on the numbers, and the goals are being met, they often don't pay too much attention to the consequences of a supervisor who is focused on process versus focused on people. Depending on the workplace culture, employees might just accept this lack of interpersonal connection as the way things are. Morale goes up and down, people get fed up and quit, injuries and sick leave increase, and maybe quality or efficiency even decreases for a time. But, if the bottom-line metrics are achieved over the long run, this type of supervisor can have a long life. I would, however, argue that enabling this supervisory style inhibits the extent to which employees and organizations can thrive versus merely survive. And I wonder why if training in civility and social competence could increase retention, engagement, and the bottom line by an average of 30 percent[24], (which is what the research says happens when organizations incorporate civility by way of socially smart best practice), wouldn't we give the supervisors some training?

You might be surprised to know that item b) above - being afraid of people as the reason some supervisors don't interact with people, is quite common. Social Anxiety Disorder (social phobia) is the third largest mental health care problem in the world today.[25] Social anxiety is the fear of social situations that involve interaction with other people. It includes the fear of

---

[24] The 30percent Solution, Bayer, Motivational Press, 2017

[25] https://socialphobia.org/social-anxiety-disorder-definition-symptoms-treatment-therapy-medications-insight-prognosis

being negatively judged and evaluated by others. It is a pervasive disorder and causes anxiety in almost all areas of a person's life. It is chronic because it does not go away on its own. The disorder is measured on a continuum and so can range anywhere from someone being shy or nervous in specific situations all the way to acute and debilitating fear about interacting with others. I'm sure you can imagine how even someone who has low-level social anxiety might opt to hide out away from people if the situation he/she is avoiding is not only social, but also stressful, high-risk, and new. In addition, many younger generations, while not scared of people, are just not as comfortable interacting face-to-face as they are communicating electronically.

The only way to offset this issue and facilitate a people-focused supervisory approach is to identify when anxiety is a legitimate issue and evaluate the extent to which the issue can be managed, e.g., with training. In some cases, it is helpful to outline expectations and set clear guidelines for face time and live interactions. And it is necessary to detail in job descriptions what tasks are required to be completed in person. Then organizations must provide appropriate training to supervisors who are by nature or habit "socially-avoidant" and the organization must allow these supervisors some time for adjustment and social skills development.

Regarding point c), a lack of skills and/or low knowledge as a reason to hide out in and of itself isn't necessarily a bad thing, for the short term anyway. Everyone starts somewhere and learning is part of the job. The problem occurs when supervisors do not acknowledge that they don't know everything. Some supervisors think they can fake it till they make it. They don't ask questions. They don't ask for help. They nod their head and say, "Yeah, yeah, I know" every time they are spoken to. They avoid the people that they are supervising because they don't understand the jobs those people do. And they hide out thinking that no one will find out that they are inexperienced as a supervisor and don't' know what they're doing.

The idea that you can fake it till you make it in manufacturing is a serious mistake. There is a lot of risk in the job. Safety is critical and you don't want to fake competency when life and limb is potentially at stake. You can maybe fake confidence for a while though. By this I mean that if you are self-assured enough to know that learning is part of the process and you allow yourself to forge ahead, anticipating you will figure things out, you will probably do okay.

If you are socially intelligent and personable, if you believe you are likeable and you adopt an air of humility, this personal confidence can serve as a precursor to competence. In my experience applying social intelligence is a very effective strategy. But it only works if you are humble enough to acknowledge the skills and contribution of others. You want to be perceived as credible such that people will listen when you speak, or so they will offer up information because they sense that you are a decent person just trying to do his/her job.

The fact is I have learned that if you are willing to ask for help, to admit when you don't know something, and to actively credit and acknowledge the people who know more than you, your job as a supervisor will be increasingly less difficult. The reality is, the production team- the workers on the floor, are often experts at their job. Many manufacturing workers are on the job for years, in fact, the manufacturing industry reported the highest median tenure among private-sector workers, with five years as the average term[26]. In my experience, about 60 percent of the production team have been on the job an average of ten years. Still, even if we accept five years as the average, imagine how well a person who has been doing the same job for eight hours a day for an estimated 1300 days. Chances are he/she knows all the nuances of every task required to do that job. That a supervisor wouldn't acknowledge this or try to leverage this resource, just doesn't make sense. Having said this, knowing the resource is there, and having the ability to tap into it are two very different things.

---

[26] https://www.rasmussen.edu/degrees/business/blog/employee-tenure-trends/

Supervisors need to build relationships so that they can access the information and supports that the production employees have. And this is where social skills are critical. Specifically, supervisors need social intelligence so that they can:

- Sense the appropriate time to approach someone
- Consider contextual aspects, e.g., deadlines, outside pressures, illness, etc
- Recognize cues that suggest the other person is willing to engage
- Send cues that build trust with the other person
- Adapt social style based on reading the cues of the other person's social style
- Apply social knowledge, e.g., pick up on and follow both written and unwritten rule

When I started working as a consultant with Civility Experts Inc. I learned a lot about Social Intelligence and Neurolinguistic Cues and Programming. Over the years I had an awareness of cues and a knack for reading people, but I didn't know the science behind it and couldn't explain to others how to build the skill. The fact is, if you are paying attention, people will tell you all kinds of things.

I have learned that it is employees' experience in a workplace that makes up what can be labeled as "organizational culture". Generally, related to paying attention to people, the overall expectations for communication, e.g., how, when, and how frequently, people at all levels of the organization interact with and speak to each other is an important part of workplace culture. A supervisor with the ability to learn about an employees' experience at work by reading verbal, nonverbal, and contextual cues (social radar) has a significant advantage. Further, a supervisor who not only observes social cues and patterns but also interprets them effectively can learn a lot about what motivates people, how high morale is, anticipate potential challenges, etc. very quickly. The problem is that many supervisors do not have well-developed social intelligence.

Key Take-Away

The role of supervisor in manufacturing is a people-focused job. At some point, you are going to have to interact face-to-face with people. Relying on phones and radios, email, and paper communication will only take you so far. You can't hide behind a clipboard and expect to earn the trust of your colleagues. You must learn to be present. You must pay attention and be able to read verbal, nonverbal, tonal, and contextual cues.

Social Competence Skill Supervisors Need: Social Intelligence – Presence

You may not know that a whopping 93 percent of communication effectiveness is determined by non-verbal cues. This means that in spite of increasing reliance on technology to do our communicating for us, talking face-to-face is more important than ever.[27] As such, if your job is to supervise people, it makes sense that you are going to need to have high social radar.

Social radar which is the ability to read nonverbal, verbal, tonal, and contextual cues is one aspect of social intelligence. Social Intelligence is one of several intelligences. For example, there is Kinesthetic Intelligence, Auditory Intelligence, Mathematical Intelligence etc., and, it should be noted that Social Intelligence is different from Emotional Intelligence. My experience has been that social intelligence is critical to long term success in life and in work. And having high social intelligence can offset deficiencies in other types of intelligence.

---

[27] https://www.thebalancecareers.com/tips-for-understanding-nonverbal-communication-1918459

In *Social IQ: The New Science of Success*, leading Social Intelligence Researcher Karl Albrecht describes social intelligence as a cluster of subskills under the acronym SPACE[28]

Skill Dimension	Involves	
S	Situational Radar (Awareness)	The ability to "read" situations, understand the social context that influences behaviour, and choose behavioural strategies that are most likely to be successful.
P	Presence	Also known as "bearing," presence is the external sense of one's self that others perceive confidence, self-respect and self-worth.
A	Authenticity	The opposite of being "phony," authenticity is a way of behaving that engenders a perception that one is honest with one's self as well as others.
C	Clarity	The ability to express one's self clearly, use language effectively, explain concepts clearly and persuade with ideas.
E	Empathy	More than just an internal sense of relatedness or appreciation for the experiences of others, empathy in this context represents the ability to create a sense of connectedness with others; to get them on your wavelength and invite them to move with and toward you rather than away and against you.

---

[28] http://karlalbrecht.com/articles/pages/socialintelligence.htm

In a manufacturing environment, these aspects of SPACE are useful to supervisors in many ways, for example:

Supervisors need situational radar (S) when:

- Learning the nuances of a new work environment
- Assessing the levels of cooperation and collaboration among and across teams
- Identifying potential interpersonal issues and/or conflict
- timing communications
- Recognizing "hot buttons" or aspects of the job or individuals that may need more supervising than others

Supervisors need to have bearing, or "presence" (P) when:

- Giving feedback
- Being perceived as credible when giving directions
- Disciplining
- Giving non-negotiable instructions

Supervisors need to be authentic (A) when:

- Building a reputation with a new team
- Building trust with peers and higher ups
- Conveying risk

Supervisors need to express themselves with clarity (C) when:

- Ensuring health and safety risks are managed
- Giving directions
- Training new skills

Supervisors need to be empathetic (E) when:

- Communicating to resolve emotional or traumatic issues, e.g., injury
- Interacting with individuals who perceive inequity or inequality
- Managing genuine "human" issues, e.g., illness, death, stress, etc.

How Do You Teach Social Intelligence?

Social competence is achieved through practice. You can read about it and learn the theory but the only way to become skilled is to deliberately put yourself in face-to-face and social settings. You must be present to the moment, that is, focused. You must set aside distractions. You must pay attention and watch body language, listen to tone of voice, etc. And then you must consider what outside or environmental factors might be influencing the behaviour you are observing. Next, you must take all that information and consider any potential biases or personal aspects that might be influencing your interpretation. And then, you can formulate an evaluation of what the cue or behaviour means.

Since I was young, I've sometimes felt like I didn't quite fit socially and some might describe me as shy in certain situations. Sometimes I would say the wrong thing, in the wrong way, to the wrong person, at the wrong time. I'm sure almost everyone has experienced this at some point. Friends and family who knew I was well-intentioned in my communications and saw that I was genuinely interested in learning about people, would gently correct me or offer suggestions as to what might be more appropriate next time. As I made my way through school and various jobs, I have adopted what I call a "reverse social engineering" technique that has been a great tool for managing the kind of communications supervisors are required to have ongoing on the job. Here is how it works.

a) Knowing that I do not want to make a social error, for example, speak when I shouldn't, I tend to hold back rather than race into communications. I wait to be approached or prompted to ask a question. I work hard to listen more than I speak.
b) When others are speaking, I pay attention and make mental notes about words they use, their postures, tone, and other nonverbal cues. I also try to note any situational aspects, E.g., do they seem distracted, and

if so, is it due always at a particular time of day? Is there something going on that would influence or cause that behaviour? Does the person exhibit those same cues when other people are around or involved or just with me?

c) If, in spite of what I feel at the time is a positive or productive interaction, a conflict, challenge, or misunderstanding occurs, for example, a conversation doesn't go the way I wanted, I try to accept that there was a disconnect without blaming or getting upset about it. For example, if the other person doesn't do what I wanted or does it differently than I expected, I acknowledge that there is a gap between what I said and what the other person heard, understood, or felt. And I set out to find out what that gap was.

d) I focus on the data. I go back in my mind and remember the body language and facial cues the person I was interacting with exhibited. I also think about any situational factors that I can remember that could have influenced the communication. I can then connect the specific gestures exhibited by that specific person as an indication that he/she did not understand me, or were intimidated, distracted, being passive aggressive, etc. And/or I can identify situational factors that were barriers to understanding.

e) Then, next time I engage with that person, I recognize those same cues and I adjust my approach and communication style until I no longer see those cues. I deliberately observe and make mental note of the cues and gestures that that individual exhibits when he/she does understand and then adjust my style and tone etc. as necessary ongoing.

Basically, I am applying a continuous improvement approach which includes implementing/completing a task (in this case an interaction), going back to assess and gather data and make observations about outcomes. Then I quantify or qualify the data and make improvements based on what was observed. This strategy works very well for people who are not socially savvy or comfortable in social settings because the learning can be achieved by bringing things back to data and observable information, e.g., you don't have to understand the meaning or emotion behind the cues and gestures, you just have to be able to notice them, document them, and then marry them up with the outcomes generated in that circumstance.

Masotti Commonsense Social Competence Strategy #3: Get Out There and Talk to People

- ☐ Always keep your head up when passing others or walking through a workspace, halls, parking lot, etc.
- ☐ Even if you don't know people, make it your habit to glance at them. Practice noticing things about people; what they're wearing, expressions, etc.
- ☐ Practice keeping an approachable, friendly look on your face.
- ☐ Be deliberate about exhibiting open postures: don't sit with your arms crossed, take your hands out of your pockets, remove sunglasses when talking to people indoors, extend an open palm for a handshake.
- ☐ When you know people (even if you don't know their names) make eye contact and smile.
- ☐ If you can't stop to talk, wave or nod hello, but don't ask a question such as, "How are you?" while you continue walking or moving.
- ☐ If you have time to stop and chat. Stop. Turn your shoulders square with the other person, greet him/her, move to within 24 inches of the other person, and engage. Set aside all other distractions while you do so.
- ☐ If you have to break eye contact or move your attention to someone or something else for a minute, e.g., check your watch, or acknowledge another person, say, "excuse me" before you do it, or say, "sorry about that" after you do it.

- ☐ As you are chatting, make a point to focus on the other person. Ask him/her questions and wait for the answers. Try to avoid talking about yourself.
- ☐ If you didn't shake hands when you greeted the person, and/or when context and culture suggest its appropriate, extend an exit handshake.
- ☐ If you are legitimately busy, don't stop and pretend to pay attention. Simply state that you are glad to see the person but are unable to visit at this time, and then wish the person a good day and move on.

"Don't mistake the devices that connect us with the moments that keep us together". – Canada GoRving ad.

Please see Chapter 11 for Sources and Resources for ongoing learning.

Chapter 4
Listen to Wise Old Men and Women

"If you are not the most experienced or the most educated person, you had better be humble enough to acknowledge this fact. And, you had better be open to learning ongoing, and to learning from others" – Christian Masotti

Years ago, I remember doing some virtual training when I worked at Ford. I think the program was called "Virtual Factory" or something like that. In any case, you make cars on a computer. You order stock and supplies etc. Things break. The line stops, there's a spill on the floor, and other scenarios that you must resolve. As I made my way through the activities, I remember seeing a character kind of in the background. It was an older man in a lab coat. The man fumbled around, bumped into things, maybe murmured or interrupted, etc., I can't remember exactly all the details, but I do remember seeing him. No one (other characters in the virtual plant) really talked to him, he was just in the background.

At the end of the online role-play, the system gives you feedback on how you completed the activities, asks you questions, offers ideas for what the best answers or solutions were and so on. At one point, it is suggested that you could have completed the tasks more easily and more quickly if you had asked this man, who was a long-term employee and who knew everything about the processes and products, questions. For some reason, that lesson stuck with me. It was an important lesson as time and time again I've learned that when it comes to manufacturing workplaces, it can be a serious mistake to ignore the learning and people resources that are often right in front of you. An important social competence strategy for supervisors is to listen to wise old men and women- and by old and wise, I mean people who have been on the job longer than you, regardless of their titles.

As a new supervisor, you need to acknowledge that you can't possibly know everything there is to know about the organization's products and processes. This is true ongoing but especially if you are new. It's also important to recognize that there probably isn't a problem or situation that hasn't happened before. While it might be new to you, there's a good chance someone around you has already been through that same scenario, or something similar. Even with this recognition, many of us still tend to dismiss peers and others who are older than we are or have been on the job longer.

It takes character to admit that you don't know everything. In manufacturing cultures where asking for help can be perceived as a sign of weakness, it also takes courage to ask questions, to admit mistakes, and to acknowledge the value of others. These are all habits of continuous learners.

One of the reasons it takes courage to build these relationships is because if your social radar is on, you will likely observe push back, resistance, and in some cases, employees will outright refuse to help you or answer questions. This can be scary for new supervisors. Try not to be afraid of these reactions. Much of the time this behaviour has nothing to do with you. For example, employees may have seen several supervisors come and go before you. Maybe they gave answers to these same questions and nothing was done. Or maybe they have been giving the answers all along and no one is listening. Maybe they didn't get a break and so are angry. Maybe they don't know the answer or just hesitate to be seeing helping you. Or maybe they disagree with you and don't feel safe or comfortable saying so. If, when you ask questions, employees seem to want to discuss, object, argue or debate, this is a good thing. Try not to immediately see it as a personal attack or interpret it as insubordination.

> In healthy companies, people debate issues. They know that smart people won't always agree. They expect dissent around any big management decision,

and they keep the lines of communication open. They don't silence people who disagree with them because they know that healthy debate is good for them and bad for their competitors.

In unhealthy companies, there is no debate. There is no dissent. If you don't toe the party line you get fired. If you can't stand the dysfunction for another minute, you bail. That's why the best employees always quit first. They have the most confidence and the most job opportunities in other firms. The fearful employees stick around. It's hard to see our own fear when we are in the middle of it.

Now that you're out of that toxic environment, look back at your fear. Don't be ashamed of it. We all feel fear at times. Pay attention to your fear so you can learn from it. [29]

The fact is, you'll have to overcome your fears about dealing with disagreement or being challenged because in most workplaces, it is the long-term employees, the people who have been doing the job for years who are the real experts. These employees know the job, the equipment, the workplace culture, the processes, the typical challenges, and almost always they also have the information, solutions, and answers that you need. In some cases, they have valid reasons for not wanting to change and/or disagreeing with something.

A lot of this information isn't recorded anywhere. You just must be humble enough to ask for it and according to the research, it is important that you do so. Some experts estimate that 25 percent of the 12 million manufacturing employees now working in the U.S. are 55 years of age or older. Replacing these people when they retire is a big problem for manufacturers because they are the most experienced and

---

[29] https://www.forbes.com/sites/lizryan/2018/03/07/the-real-reason-great-employees-quit-and-bad-employees-get-promoted/#33dece40880d

skilled people working in a manufacturing plant—and the knowledge base they've built over decades will go with them when they retire[30].

If a supervisor is new to an industry, a company or a workforce, one way to expedite learning is to tap into the knowledge base of the people that he/she is supervising. This is called tribal knowledge. Tribal knowledge is any unwritten information that is not commonly known by others within a company. This term is used most when referencing information that may need to be known by others in order to produce quality products or services. [31]

Although you may have great skills in managing people or great knowledge of the product or service you are supervising, a supervisor must acknowledge that the combined experience and knowledge of all the people they are supervising will always be greater than what one supervisor can achieve alone. This scenario is an opportunity that the supervisor needs to value. For example, the 40 people on an assembly line or office environment performing 40 individual skills/job tasks for the last few years, or even decades, know all the little idiosyncrasies of their individual jobs and much of this isn't captured in standard operating procedures or job descriptions. It's impossible for a supervisor to know all those details.

Uncovering all the hidden tribal knowledge will help continuous improvement. The question is, how do you provide an environment where your employees are willing to share that information with you? Employees will share this knowledge if they feel valued, respected, trust you as a supervisor, and feel confident that this information will be used to make their work experience, and the experience of others better.

---

[30] https://www.industryweek.com/talent/recruiting-retention/article/22007278/a-strategy-to-capture-tribal-knowledge

[31] https://www.isixsigma.com/dictionary/tribal-knowledge/

Creating an environment where these people resources can be leveraged can be of tremendous benefit to supervisors because, these employees:

- Have a lot of very specific tribal knowledge, e.g., about fixing old equipment
- Have survived all kinds of changes that occurred in the workplace and can share lessons learned
- Are wise about how to manage oneself in that workplace culture e.g., they know the unwritten rules
- Have insight about personnel, leadership, customers, suppliers
- Have social credibility and sometimes influence, e.g., they have earned the trust of their peers

These people resources are often right in front of us. And so, given the proximity and knowing they are so valuable, why do we still ignore them? There are a lot of reasons, including:

a) We assume we have new or current education or information that the other person does not

b) We have a bias about age, e.g., we think someone older must be slower or stuck in his/her ways, or not up to date on information

c) We presume that people who have heavy accents or speak different languages are not smart or that we won't understand them

d) We assume contention, that is, these people see me as the enemy, they won't help me so why ask

e) We avoid people who seem stressed or troubled or in a bad mood, e.g., we are self-focused

f) We make assumptions about culture, e.g., those people don't respect authority, those people are always pro-union, etc.

g) We don't want to let the other guy be right, e.g., if they already think they know more than we do

h) We are embarrassed about what we don't know

i) We honestly think we know everything, or at least enough

j) We legitimately are afraid to approach others

k) There legitimately hasn't been an appropriate time to approach, e.g., workplace challenges, crisis to manage, etc.

l) There are physical barriers or protocols e.g., chain of command, etc., that prevent us from approaching

m) The other person/persons have made it clear that they are unwilling to share/help

n) We really don't care, e.g., we are only concerned about getting by, doing the minimum and it doesn't matter in the end if things are done the easy or most cost-effective way

o) We are afraid of reprisal, e.g., someone will tell others, or we will be punished for not knowing something

p) We honestly don't know where to start, e.g., what questions to ask

q) The workplace culture's unwritten rules prohibit asking subordinates for help

r) There legitimately is no time to ask questions or get help, e.g., health or safety issue and you must make a quick decision using the information you have

s) We lack humility, plain and simple

While some of the reasons listed have applied to me at various points in my career, I think, for the most part, I have always had a natural tendency to respect and reach out to people on the job. Especially older people. I think it's because I grew up in a family where elders were respected. Growing up, my grandfather was one of my most favorite people. He and my uncles were mentors to me. My grandfather taught me to appreciate what you have and to be humble. He worked in manufacturing most of his life and he lived a quiet, simple life and focused on being a good person and providing for his family. I credit my father with giving me my thirst for knowledge. He always encouraged my brothers and me to be curious, to find information and to ask questions. In hindsight, I see how all these family influencers were social mentors to me. While what they taught me is maybe more accurately described as wisdom, I have been able to apply a lot of what they taught me in my work life as well as in my personal life.

I was fortunate enough to have mentors on the job too. One piece of advice given to me early on, one that I share with all new supervisors I train, is that you need to have a big brother or sister on the job. You need to have one person you can trust, someone who understands your role, someone who is forthright and honest with you. It's ideal if this person is a higher up, like maybe a manager, but all you need is one trusted ally. Having this mentor can make all the difference. (And this mentor usually knows, or can access, a lot of tribal knowledge).

This mentor can offer support to you when you need it and can also be supportive when you make mistakes. The mentor can protect you from non-standard conditions or variability in day to day activities. The manager/mentor supports you and looks after you because he/she sees that you are asking questions, valuing his/her experience, building relationships with your employees, and doing all your due diligence during your workday.

To be able to draw on experience, to extract wisdom from a mentor and others, and to ask questions are all aspects of being a continuous learner. Being a continuous learner is an important skill for supervisors.

Key Take-Away

If you are not the most experienced or the most educated person, you had better be humble enough to acknowledge this fact. And, you had better be open to learning ongoing, and to learning from others. Be humble, be present, ask questions, pay attention to the answers, and you can learn almost everything you need to be successful as a supervisor.

Communication Skill: Continuous Learning

To learn on the job, you must be able to learn continuously, this includes building connections and trust with people suffice to get information from them. Continuous Learning includes learning from your own experiences, seeking information, asking questions, and learning from others.

How Do You Teach Continuous Learning?

Continuous learning is learning how to learn[32]. If you are humble enough to admit that you don't know everything and smart enough to acknowledge that you need to rely on mentors and others, every day presents new opportunities to learn.

To take advantage of these opportunities you need to develop our continuous learning skills. I encourage supervisors to consciously and consistently plan to learn something every day. And at the end of the day reflect on what you've learned. Continuous learners engage in the following behaviours on a regular basis, how many apply to you? Do you:

---

[32] https://www.skillscompetencescanada.com/en/essential-skills/what-are-the-nine-essential-skills/#continuouslearning

- ☐ Think in different ways
- ☐ Self-reflect
- ☐ Inquire and ask questions
- ☐ Seek feedback from others
- ☐ Draw conclusions
- ☐ Gather insights
- ☐ Conceptualize the learning process
- ☐ Organize our learning
- ☐ Participate in training
- ☐ Set goals
- ☐ Actively engage in gathering knowledge
- ☐ Understand our learning style
- ☐ Practice applying what we learn
- ☐ Adapt and change
- ☐ Improve ourselves on an ongoing basis

The more you engage in continuous learning, the more confident you will become. You will also increase your overall adaptive capacity, your competence, and your performance. All these benefits can increase your future opportunities and your personal credibility. Continuous Learning can also bring measurable benefits to your organization. For example, in organizations that support a culture of continuous learning, there are often higher levels of engagement, greater accountability, increased co-operation, high productivity, and reduced turnover- this due in part to increased trust and a mutual understanding by both the employer and the employee that continuous learning increases employability[33].

In addition to the people you can access for support and information, there are lots of underutilized continuous learning tools available on the job. Many supervisors see the tools below as merely reporting or tracking documents, they don't recognize their value from a learning perspective:

---

[33] WEM, Change Readiness Certificate Program Research, 2017, Bayer et al.

1. Daily logs – you can learn a lot about the common conditions, the routines, the general communication style of colleagues, etc. and if you are paying attention, you can also pick up on patterns. E.g., logs should include metrics charts that show goals and output, downtime and so on
2. Incident reports – you can learn about existing problems, try to discern root cause, review how problems were solved; look for patterns and triggers
3. SOPs – (standard operating procedures) can tell you a lot about the pace of change, team readiness, and resilience, e.g., how often are SOPs updated? When was the last time study done? Who wrote the SOP? (hopefully someone who completes that task on the job contributed)
4. Safety records – can hint at underlying equipment issues or process faults
5. Sick day and/or Time off requests – you can get a sense of overall morale and stressors as well as stress times

Another key thing when learning is not to make assumptions about the information you are taking in. You must confirm that the data is accurate and factual. You must check sources. You can't always be sure that a person perceived to be credible is giving credible information. You must pay attention, focus, read, listen to understand, and be curious. There is no harm in asking questions, in fact, it's a good idea to get in the habit of always asking a few questions, just monitor your tone as you do so.

One trick to managing the tone when questioning is to try not to use the word "I" in your statements. For example:

Instead of: "I was wondering if you could help me with X"

Say: "Would you be able to give some feedback on X"

or "What do you think is the best approach to fixing X?"

or "You are the expert with X, what do you think happened?"

Another approach is to ask for help but give the other person option about when and how to help. For example:

Instead of: "You are going to have to fix X by 3:30"

Say: "What do you think it will take for you to be able to fix X?"

We discuss tone and questioning in more detail in Chapter 6.

Masotti Commonsense Social Competence Strategy #4
Apply Continuous Learning to Connect with People

- ☐ Treat people with respect from the beginning so that when you need to approach them for help, they see you as someone they can trust who values them
- ☐ Assume that someone, at some time, somewhere has experienced this same situation
- ☐ Assume that you are not the only person to have an idea
- ☐ Always ask the people doing the job, ask them directly, face-to-face
- ☐ Approach people at the appropriate time
- ☐ Be respectful in your tone, don't assume people have an obligation to help you just because you are a supervisor
- ☐ Ask targeted questions e.g., not open-ended
- ☐ Admit you need help
- ☐ Listen for answers- don't interrupt, don't criticize or apply your personal biases, opinions or beliefs
- ☐ Don't dismiss anyone, you never know what information will be useful down the road, even if the information being shared at the time is not relevant, use the interaction as an opportunity to build rapport and trust
- ☐ Consider that one person may not have all the answers, but the collective probably does
- ☐ Acknowledge the sharing and the information, let the person sharing with you know you appreciate their help

- ☐ Give credit when you use the information down the road
- ☐ Share the information with others, e.g., don't hoard it now that you have it
- ☐ Avoid going back to the same person more than once, this can cause strain within the team. Instead, build a relationship with each member of the team, this builds credibility

Please see Chapter 11 for Sources and Resources for ongoing learning.

Chapter 5
ALWAYS Tell the Truth

"In my experience, supervisors with consistent character will often outperform supervisors who are smarter or work harder. This is because consistency of character builds trust and trust is critical to success in any leadership role". – Christian Masotti

If there is one thing I can't tolerate it's lying. In workplaces, lying equals risk. That someone would lie shows blatant disregard for their coworkers, for safety, and for profitability. It's immature, and it's irresponsible. Whether the lie is about a little thing, like why someone isn't coming in to work, or a big thing, like having made a critical error that required stopping the production line and cost the company tens of thousands of dollars, I don't like lying and I don't typically accept it from those I supervise.

Honesty is an element of character. Moral character is an evaluation of an individual's stable moral qualities. The concept of character can imply a variety of attributes including the existence or lack of virtues such as empathy, courage, fortitude, honesty, and loyalty, or of good behaviours or habits[34]. While most people understand honesty as a value or virtue, I suggest that in the workplace, being honest translates to an ability to convey transparency, and to exhibit integrity (living one's values). Honest communication is also an important aspect of accountability.

I used to be surprised how frequently people proport to be honest and at the same time adopt lying as a habit. But, over the years I have come to understand this behaviour, not that I condone it, but I do understand it. While on the surface I agree that dishonesty is dishonesty, plain and simple, it is true that in real life we can sometimes justify dishonesty by differentiating

---

[34] https://en.wikipedia.org/wiki/Moral_character

between telling a harmless untruth, and willful deceit.

I, and I believe most people, strive to be honest. Statistically speaking though, we are all liars. **Researchers** estimate the average person lies a minimum of once to twice per day[35]. If you don't believe me, ask yourself these questions:

- *Do you ever give people compliments that aren't completely genuine?*
- *Have you told someone you were doing well when you were exhausted and having a terrible week?*
- *Do you ever **tell people you are busy** to avoid having to talk to them for an extended period of time or do something with them?*

The above examples are dishonest, and technically lies, but fall into the category I would call harmless untruths. Often these untruths are told to protect someone else's feelings or to withhold information we have no business sharing. Myself included I don't know anyone who can say they have never told a white lie to protect someone.

The unfortunate fact is that many manufacturing cultures require that supervisors lie. For the most part, the lying isn't malicious. It's usually to protect the organization. Sometimes decision-makers need to hold back sharing information with the shareholders for a short time. Or, because there has historically been conflict based on diverse interests between union and management in manufacturing, management might hold off telling whole truths to buy time and avoid upsetting production. As a supervisor, telling half-truths due to one's authority to share certain information, is actually part of the job. But, even when dishonesty seems required, any time there is a perceived lack of transparency or someone gets caught in a lie, no matter how small, building and maintaining

---

[35] https://www.scienceofpeople.com/9-things-know-liars/

trust can be very difficult.

The frequency of the dishonesty matters as well. For example, a supervisor might be forgiven for lying once if the lie is discovered to be an action predicated on accountability. However, if there is a pattern of deception, that supervisor is going to have a hard time earning the trust of his/her team, regardless of the reasons they are lying. This is why always telling the truth, and where possible always telling the whole truth, is a social competence strategy for supervisors.

Interestingly, research shows that the majority of lies are told by the same, small group of people known as 'prolific' liars. In the study *Variance in the Prevalence of Lying*, researchers created a statistical model for distinguishing prolific liars from the everyday or 'normal' liar.

Here's are qualities of a prolific liar:

- Prolific liars are those who report that they tell five or more lies per day.
- Prolific liars tend to be younger, male and have higher occupational statuses.
- They are likely to lie the most to their partners and children.
- They are more likely than the average person to believe that lying is acceptable in some circumstances.
- They are less likely to lie because of concern for others and more likely to lie for their own self-interest, such as to protect a secret.
- Prolific liars tell five and a half lies for every one white lie told by an average person.
- They tell 19.1 lies for everyone big lie told by an average person[36].

In workplace environments, supervisors must learn to spot

---

[36] https://journals.sagepub.com/doi/abs/10.1177/0261927X14528804

prolific liars. Sadly, research suggests that 80 percent of people are dissatisfied with their jobs.[37] However, the majority of those people have to keep their jobs and so the day to day necessity for seemingly harmless little white lies about how you feel, what your goals are, etc., are frequent, and when this type of lying becomes a habit, it's almost a gateway behaviour to more dangerous lying. Obviously, supervisors should NOT be prolific liars themselves. Prolific liars are often motivated to lie due to the reasons below. I'm sure you can understand why in manufacturing environments where safety is a priority, the lies these people tell are potentially very dangerous. If the individual is an influencer or perceived to be a "good guy", he/she can cause all kinds of havoc.

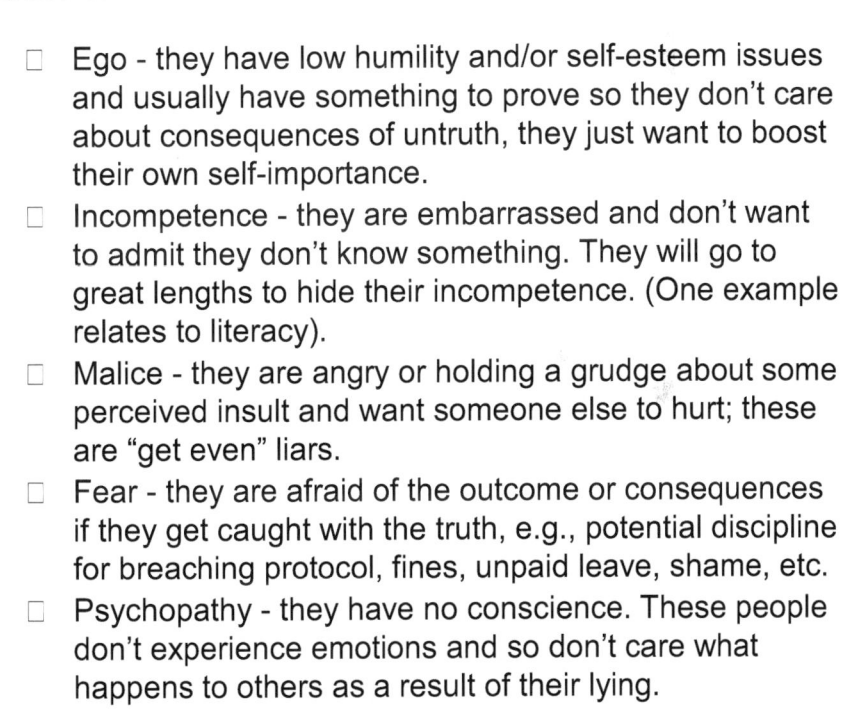

- Ego - they have low humility and/or self-esteem issues and usually have something to prove so they don't care about consequences of untruth, they just want to boost their own self-importance.
- Incompetence - they are embarrassed and don't want to admit they don't know something. They will go to great lengths to hide their incompetence. (One example relates to literacy).
- Malice - they are angry or holding a grudge about some perceived insult and want someone else to hurt; these are "get even" liars.
- Fear - they are afraid of the outcome or consequences if they get caught with the truth, e.g., potential discipline for breaching protocol, fines, unpaid leave, shame, etc.
- Psychopathy - they have no conscience. These people don't experience emotions and so don't care what happens to others as a result of their lying.

The research supports the assumption that a person who is a prolific liar is a high risk. For example., research validates that individuals who score low on Honesty and Humility

---

[37] https://www2.deloitte.com/us/en/pages/center-for-the-edge/articles/shift-index-worker-passion-survey.html

Assessments are more likely to engage in unethical business practices, and to more likely take health and safety risks, even towards fellow employees[38]. A common assessment (used by many large organizations as a screening tool) is the HEXACO model which assesses six broad personality factors:

- ***Honesty-Humility (H):***
  - **Facets:** Sincerity, Fairness, Greed Avoidance, Modesty
  - **Adjectives:** Sincere, honest, faithful, loyal, modest/unassuming *versus* sly, deceitful, greedy, pretentious, hypocritical, boastful, pompous
- ***Emotionality (E):***
  - **Facets:** Fearfulness, Anxiety, Dependence, Sentimentality
  - **Adjectives:** Emotional, oversensitive, sentimental, fearful, anxious, vulnerable *versus* brave, tough, independent, self-assured, stable
- ***Extraversion (X):***
  - **Facets:** Social Self-Esteem, Social Boldness, Sociability, Liveliness
  - **Adjectives:** Outgoing, lively, extraverted, sociable, talkative, cheerful, active *versus* shy, passive, withdrawn, introverted, quiet, reserved
- ***Agreeableness (A):***
  - **Facets:** Forgivingness, Gentleness, Flexibility, Patience
  - **Adjectives:** patient, tolerant, peaceful, mild, agreeable, lenient, gentle *versus* ill-tempered, quarrelsome, stubborn, choleric

---

[38] Lee, K.; Ashton, M.C. (2004). "The HEXACO Personality Inventory: A New Measure of the Major Dimensions of Personality". *Multivariate Behavioural Research.* **39** (2): 329–358

- **Conscientiousness (C):**
  - **Facets:** Organization, Diligence, Perfectionism, Prudence
  - **Adjectives:** organized, disciplined, diligent, careful, thorough, precise *versus* sloppy, negligent, reckless, lazy, irresponsible, absent-minded
- **Openness to Experience (O):**
  - **Facets:** Aesthetic Appreciation, Inquisitiveness, Creativity, Unconventionality[39]
  - **Adjectives:** intellectual, creative, unconventional, innovative, ironic *versus* shallow, unimaginative, conventional

Key Take-Away

Consistent character, e.g., being honest, will often outperform competence. This is because consistency of character builds trust. When you have trust, people will work with you. You don't have to be the smartest or the most skilled when you have the cooperation of your work team and you can benefit from the competency of the collective.

Social Competence Skill Supervisors Need: Honesty

If you take some time to review the HEXACO factors and facets listed above, you can see how honesty and humility would tie to social success. If you are not honest, it is very difficult to build and maintain trust. People get a sense of your values based on how you treat them and at work a large part of this is based on communication skills. Consistency is important and so it can take time to build trust.

---

[39] Lee, K.; Ashton, M.C. (2004). "The HEXACO Personality Inventory: A New Measure of the Major Dimensions of Personality". Multivariate Behavioural Research. **39** (2): 329–358.

One lie can destroy a thousand truths. It will take weeks or months or possibly never to gain an employee or manager's trust again. If there is some information that is pending or is confidential that cannot be revealed, just be upfront with the employee and tell them exactly why you cannot commit to full responses to their questions at the present time. Don't be vague or tell half-truths.

What a trustworthy supervisor does is build a pattern of transparency or at least honesty where he/she can't be transparent. You want your team to be able to see that historically, your habit is to give as much information as you can when it is available and appropriate to give out. That way employees get used to the fact that you never hide important information or make decisions with hidden information or an agenda. Remember, all it takes is one lie to break trust. And it doesn't matter if you are lying about what you did on Friday night or what brand of paper the copy machine takes, any lie, about any topic can be perceived as reason to doubt everything else you might have said that came before the lie, and anything you say that comes after the lie.

I can say with confidence that supervisors who are not perceived as trustworthy by their teams will not have an easy time doing their job. It is trust that enables supervisors to achieve:

- Cooperative attitude from others
- Quick responses when you need them
- Honest responses from people who don't have a technical obligation to help you
- Fair treatment from others
- Back up, e.g., people will defend you to others
- Extra effort with no expectations of "owing something" when you need supports
- 3rd party endorsement, that is, positive reputation by word of mouth

Civility Experts Inc. CEO Lew Bayer suggests that there are at least three different types of honesty. These are:

- "Social honesty" which is when a person says what is perceived to be the right thing in a certain context, e.g., when it isn't polite to tell the truth, or when telling the truth is not politically correct or could harm social impression or status.
- "Righteous honesty" which is when someone is taking an indignant or defensive stance and so blurts out hurtful honesty, e.g., tells truth about someone else's actions as a means of deflecting from their own dishonesty.
- "Authentic honesty" which is when a person tells the truth because being honest is his/her core value and doing so is the right and good thing to do. In this case, though, partly because the truth-telling is values based, the truth-teller considers the *way* the truth comes out, e.g., he/she considers how to soften the blow or tells the truth in a private setting at an appropriate time, gives the listener some warning, etc.

**Integrity (values in practice) +
Human-kindness (intention to exhibit respect) +
Compassion (recognition that the truth sometimes hurts)
= Authentic Honesty[40]**

The idea is that for honesty to benefit another person (and not just be a means of alleviating guilt or obligation on the part of the truth-teller) we must consider our intentions and also consider the impact of the truth.

How Do You Teach Honesty?
Honesty is a personal standard that influences how people make decisions. It is a value that makes up in part who a person is, his/her character.

---

[40] *Human-kindness*, Bayer and Moore, Propriety Publishing, 2020

For example, it might be expected that a person of character holds personal values such as honesty, equality, responsibility, integrity., etc. You can't force people to be honest and you can't dictate personal values. But you can encourage people to be honest by teaching them the consequences of dishonesty. And at work, you can sometimes obligate honesty under the label of "transparency". You can also require honest communication as part of communication plans or workplace codes of conduct. For example, you can require that certain information is, or isn't, made public or shared.

Further, because we know that being honest is one way to build trust and that building trust is critical to building collaborative work relationships, we can include "building trust" as a measurable aspect of a supervisor's performance. As such, supervisors need to be able to utilize different communication strategies for conveying honesty and this includes knowing how to build trust even when dishonesty (harmless untruths) is required as part of the job.

One strategy for teaching trust-building is to teach people to monitor (and read in others) gestures, words, and nonverbal cues that are known to indicate honesty. Supervisors who know these cues can monitor their own expressions so that they are perceived to be honest, or at least they are not perceived as dishonest, and they can observe signs of dishonesty when exhibited by their team members.

Significantly, about 55 percent of overall communication is nonverbal, and only 5-7 percent of that nonverbal communication is deliberate[41]. As a result, what people do versus what they say is often a reflection of what they really think or feel.

---

[41] Workplace language and Literacy Program by the Commonwealth through the Department of Education Training and Youth Affairs 25 October 2001

And so being able to read nonverbal cues is one way to assess honesty.

NON VERBAL COMMUNICATION

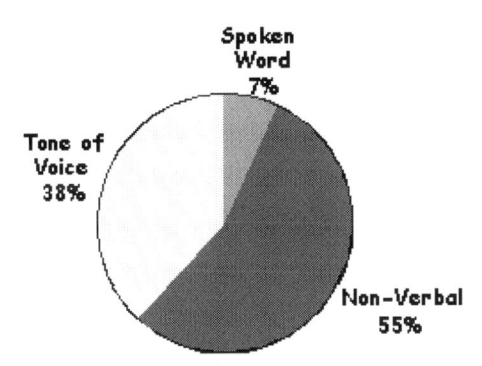

- Spoken Word 7%
- Tone of Voice 38%
- Non-Verbal 55%

When you are interacting with people and you want to know for sure that they are paying attention, listening, or thinking about what you are saying, watch for these cues.

Signs that you have someone's attention: (maybe that he/she trusts you or is being forthright with you)

- Smiling
- Nodding
- Raising eyebrows
- Saying, "Yes, please go on…"
- Leaning forward
- Listening actively
- Interrupting or finishing sentences out of excitement or interest

Signs that someone is losing interest: (potentially distracted, making up a story in his/her head, not comfortable and needing to escape)

- Wandering gaze, e.g., looking over your shoulder, not making eye contact, looking down or at their watch
- Fidgeting
- Pursing lips or giving a closed mouth smile

- Whispering or doing something other than listening to you
- Yawning or stretching
- Interrupting abruptly
- Changing the subject

Signs that someone is uncomfortable or feeling awkward: (maybe a hint that you should consider the timing of your being honest with him/her, and/or maybe hints that he/she is avoiding you or being dishonest)

- Pacing
- Rising or shifting away from you
- Leaving the area or room completely
- Fidgeting
- Lowering head
- Avoiding eye contact
- Rounding shoulders, e.g., showing a closed posture
- Blushing
- Sweating profusely
- Looking up or away
- Trembling
- Complaining of nausea or headache
- Coughing or clearing throat incessantly
- Talking too much or not at all
- Eating or drinking or avoiding eating or drinking, e.g., when doing so would be appropriate
- Pausing or hesitating
- Stating he/she doesn't remember
- Telling jokes or using humor inappropriately
- Trying to create a distraction
- Repeating him/herself

Signs that someone does not believe or is not "buying in" (e.g., maybe they think you are lying):

- Repeating themselves, "saying, "yeah, yeah...." Or "sure, sure, okay...yeah"

- Saying, "yes" with their mouth but their body language says "no"
- Avoiding asking any questions at all, signaling that they've already made up their minds
- Crossing arms

Signs that someone is not being entirely honest: (may be discomfort with the setting as well)

- Changing pitch of voice, rate of speech or volume of speech
- Hesitating when speaking
- Decreasing or increasing eye contact.
- Moving hands to cover eyes or mouth
- Moving hands, feet or legs.
- Twitching of eye (s)
- Clenching of jaw
- Smiling with a closed mouth
- Saying things that don't make sense or suddenly changing the subject

In environments where there is a perceived culture of mistrust or dishonesty seems to be the habit, another useful strategy for building trust is to build your own little island of truthful communication. The idea is to set a new standard. Start with small promises, e.g., if someone asks for gloves and you say you will get them, get the gloves. No matter what, deliver on your promise. No matter how small, don't make promises you can't keep. And if you can't make a promise, don't. But where possible at least give the reasons why you cannot promise something. For example, "I cannot promise you will get the day off because there are 5 people ahead of you who asked for that same date, but I will submit your request."

Sometimes mistrust is a result of fear of the unknown. When people hear nothing or when communications are spare, they tend to assume that no news is bad news and/or that something is being kept from them.

Keep employees updated, follow through on getting them the information they need to feel comfortable. If you said you'd have an answer by a certain time, make sure you get back to them. The sooner you can deliver, the better- but if you can't deliver in a timely way, at least have the courage to explain why and keep your team updated. Teach them that they can trust you to share the information they need and want.

You can teach personal trust by taking ownership of promises, communication, and outcomes. When you can't deliver, don't pass the buck or throw someone else under the bus, take responsibility for the outcome and show your team that you can be counted on whether the outcome is good or bad. While it is sometimes difficult to follow up when you know you are letting someone down or you don't have control over a situation, it's your willingness to be truthful even when it is hard to do that will build your credibility. Similarly, don't freak out when others find the courage to come to you with the truth, even when that truth is bad news. Stay calm, acknowledge the information, thank the other person for telling the truth, and then take some time to devise a response or solution.

When you need to uncover the truth, an important thing to learn is that people who want to lie will actively seek reasons not to be honest. Try not to give them reasons. For example: Ask specific questions. Some dishonest people will use the fact that you didn't ask a specific question as a rationale for not telling the truth. If I ask someone, "Have you observed Dan behaving irrationally today?" The other person potentially says to him/herself, "I saw Dan sitting in the corner crying, but I'm not telling you that, besides, who is to say crying is irrational?" Whereas if you had asked, "What specifically did you see Dan doing today? Or, "Did you see Dan crying in the lunchroom today?", the other person must either outright lie, or he/she has to state that Dan was seen crying.

Another helpful strategy for teaching how to build trust is to explain the consequences of lying to people, for example, "...in the real world of work, what you intended to happen-that is what you wished, hoped, meant, imagined, planned etc., e.g., rationalizing a white lie) is not terribly relevant. What you are going to be held accountable for the impact of your words and actions." [42] This means that if you held back information, told a piece of the truth, or lied, even if you were well-intentioned in doing so, at the end of the day, if someone gets hurt, if there are production issues or consequences resulting from that dishonesty, you will have breached a trust and why you did it won't change the outcome or help you recoup diminished credibility or reputation.

Lastly, you cannot assume that everyone values the truth or that everyone defines his/her values as you do. For example, "integrity", "honesty", "respect", these values can mean different things to different people, and they can look very different in practice. You can't know someone's motivation for saying or doing something unless you ask him/her. And remember, sometimes good people make bad decisions or do dishonest things. Try not to judge too harshly until you have all the facts. Unfortunately, honesty at work can be a tricky thing, what is the right thing to do or say at the right time is not always obvious or black and white. You must teach people to be forgiving. Allow people to be human. Recognize that trust happens on a continuum and that it can vary with context. For example, I can trust someone to follow safety rules at work, but that doesn't mean I am going to trust that same person with my bank card and PIN. When you don't understand why someone was dishonest, you must ask him/her, and you must consider all the influencing factors that might have led to his/her decision.

Masotti Commonsense Social Competence Strategy #5 – Always Tell the Truth

If you want to build trust, here are some communication habits you should adopt:

---

[42] Lew Bayer, Civility at Work, 2018

- Make a point to be honest with everyone- not just some people
- Be consistent, e.g., always tell the truth- don't pick and choose when to be honest
- Be honest when delivering both good and bad news
- Be direct, tell the whole truth versus a piece or version of the truth, e.g., instead of saying you are being fired for lateness, an indirect version, is saying, "You know, lateness is one of the metrics we watch."
- Assume the best of people, but don't immediately trust everything people say, ask strategic questions
- Look people in the eye when you are communicating the truth
- Be deliberate in your communication- choose your words carefully and say exactly what you mean, don't sugarcoat or be vague
- Avoid pretending you have authority or power you don't have- be honest about your abilities and influence
- Do your due diligence before making promises- ensure you can follow through before you say what you can and will do
- Pick an appropriate time to be truthful
- Consider privacy and confidentiality
- Monitor your tone, e.g., don't be harsh
- Avoid apologizing for telling the truth, e.g., "I'm sorry to have to tell you X, but…"
- Give people a minute to absorb what you are telling them
- Keep being truthful, even when others are dishonest, and/or even when no one seems to notice. People do notice, and there is often documentation to support your efforts

One lie can destroy a thousand truths. – C. Masotti

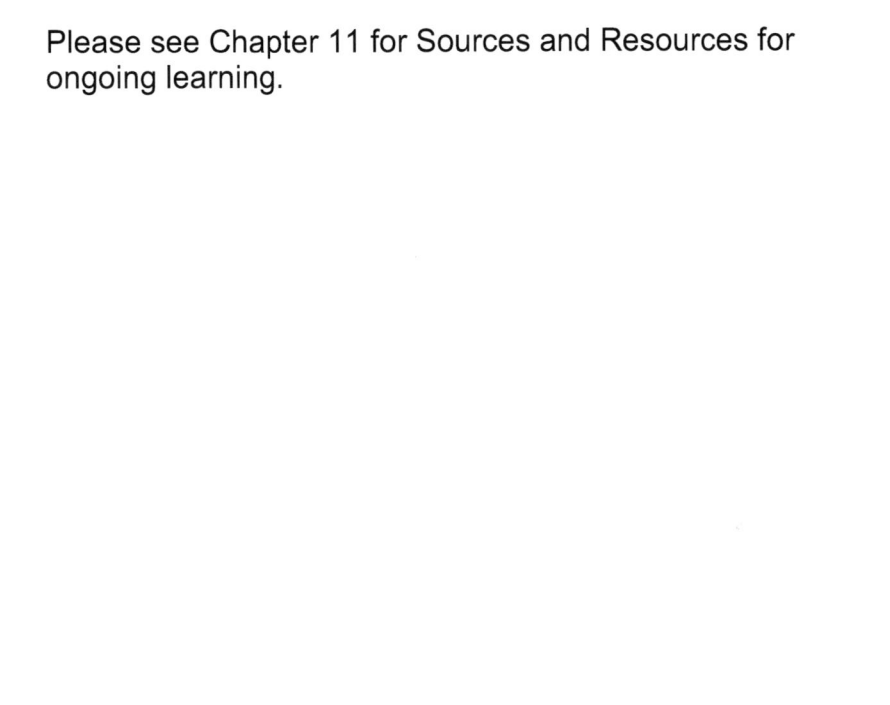

Please see Chapter 11 for Sources and Resources for ongoing learning.

Chapter 6
Tell Me What You Want (What You Really, Really Want)

> "*If you actually pay attention, if you go into situations and interactions with the intention of being of service to someone, and you ask strategic questions, and then watch and listen, people will almost always tell you what they want, even if they don't realize they are doing it*". – Christian Masotti

Over the years I can't tell you how frequently I have heard upper management or workplace trainers tell supervisors that if they want their teams to communicate and/or collaborate, they need to "build relationships" with them. I agree. It's true, you need to build relationships. But aside from saying, "Just get out there and talk to people", "Take time to get to know the people you work with", or "You have to build trust", there is very little meaningful strategy or skill taught.

How do you build trust?

How do you build rapport?

How do you get people to share information that you need?

How do you get people, who have no incentive to do so, to offer up answers to problems that you can't solve without their support?

Robin Sharma, considered a titan in the personal development world, suggests that "being a great leader, even when you don't have a title, comes down to your human connections."[43] Sharma suggests that the way you connect to others is via deep listening. I completely agree that success as a leader comes down to making human connections, but I would argue that "deep" listening which involves taking time to get to know

---

[43] https://www.youtube.com/watch?v=UvcgKWt_wos

someone on a very personal level isn't always an effective approach for building connections in manufacturing environments.

You can listen to people's personal histories, stories, anecdotes, feelings, problems, and opinions all day long, and do so under the guise of building relationships, but what you hear may or may not be pertinent to the job you are trying to do. Listening just for the sake of listening can be a huge time waster and quite frankly, manufacturing environments don't often lend themselves to uninterrupted, barrier free, opportunities for supervisors to engage in deep listening. Further, most manufacturing cultures don't really support this approach which is perceived by many long-timers in the field as weak or soft.

Of course, there is something to be said for the value of small talk. For example, if you are observing body language and listening, you can learn a lot about people even when they are talking about the weather, or their family, their opinions about the news, etc. But in high-stress, time-pressured environments like manufacturing I would NOT encourage supervisors to engage in personal chit chat with their team beyond general greetings and general acknowledgment of personal statements made by others. While supervisors should be friendly, it's not a good idea to be overly familiar with their team as this can create problems in high stakes situations where credibility and trust are critical – employees need to know that they can trust their supervisor to act like a leader versus acting like a friend when the S%*#! hits the fan.

When safety is at issue, it's best not to engage in personal conversations. If you are not sure how people will respond, e.g., even a joke can have impacts you don't expect, and if you don't know their triggers and hot buttons, potentially evoking unpredictable emotions creates unnecessary risk and is generally a bad idea.

Another reason that supervisors should not engage in small

talk as a rapport and trust building strategy is based on an interesting study by Microsoft. The research suggests that the average human being now has an attention span of eight seconds. This is a sharp decrease from the average attention span of 12 seconds in the year 2000. More shocking, perhaps, is the fact that research from Jampp found that human attention span decreases by a whopping 88 percent every year[44].

Take a minute to soak this in and think carefully about the implications of this fact for supervisors who, if they are doing their job properly, rely heavily on face-to-face communications that involve paying attention. Consider as well that in manufacturing environments, there are additional factors that are potential barriers to paying attention such as:

- Constant noise
- Physical barriers, e.g., constant movement and distracting equipment
- Time constraints, e.g., having less than 8 seconds to interact
- Social discomfort, e.g., social anxiety disorders and people not comfortable interacting face-to-face
- Organizational culture aspects, e.g., unwritten rules about interacting
- Physiological issues, e.g., "hangry", tired, stressed
- Personal issues, e.g., lack of respect or trust, for example between management and union
- Cultural differences, e.g., variance in verbal and nonverbal cues that indicate paying attention

When time is limited, safety is the priority, there are all kinds of

---

[44] https://www.cision.com/us/2018/01/declining-attention-killing-content-marketing-strategy/

barriers to communication, and you know the people you are interacting with have short attention spans, you need to get right to the point. Supervisors should focus on conveying the most important message first and communicate it in the clearest and simplest way.

The most important message usually relates to:

- A task or process that needs to be completed
- A problem that needs to be solved
- A question for which the supervisor needs an answer
- An issue or information relevant to the listener, e.g., something that impacts him/her such as a schedule change

So, rather than encourage or initiate personal conversations or dialogue that doesn't relate to the job at hand, the strategy supervisors need to employ to control the communication is to ask strategic and timely questions. Then, you watch, wait, and YES, YOU LISTEN but the intention of the listening is to – and this is key- ease the experience of the other person, that is, make his/her job easier. You do this by fostering clarity of direction, confirming understanding, and being transparent about wanting to problem-solve – in civility training, we call this "end in mind listening". With "end in mind" listening you know in advance of the conversation what you need to happen after the communication. This is goal-directed communication. By asking strategic questions, you can control to a point how much time you spend in the interaction and you can often narrow down the type of information you get. You try not to assume or guess the responses of others, and you still have to be open-minded, but you do have a plan of sorts before you engage. By using this approach, you will usually get the answers you need. And you will usually get them quickly and precisely. At the same time, you can build trust because you:

- Are forthright about why you are engaging e.g., you are not pretending to be interested personally, the fact is supervisors need to maintain a certain degree of

separation from their team – this enables them to give directives and be trusted in crisis or safety situations.
- Are going into the interacting assuming the best of the other person, you recognize him/her as a valued resource and so you approach with a respectful tone, intending to somehow make that person's job easier – ease his/her experience.
- Are not wasting the employee's time, e.g., they have a job to do and in manufacturing, schedules are tight, there is no time to waste.
- Eliminate the guesswork, e.g., employees don't have to wonder what the real reason is you are talking to them, they know you aren't trying to catch them in a lie, or embarrass them, or parent them, they learn that every time you communicate with them, there is a specific work-related purpose.
- Vary the end in mind, e.g., sometimes your goal is to give accolades or support or positive feedback, you are not always giving directives or assigning tasks so the communication is still end in mind and work-related, but it's not always negative or adding pressure.
- Give time after asking your question(s) for the other person to respond, don't jump to conclusions, and focus on gathering facts and data.
- Treat every employee the same, e.g., you are not chummy with one person or using a different approach with some people and not others, this builds your credibility as someone who is fair and values people equally.
- Can focus on facts and data and competence, e.g., when you remove the personal aspect, you can eliminate much of the emotion and as stated above, emotionality creates risk in environments where safety is the priority.

Key Take-Away

If you actually pay attention, if you go into situations and interactions with the intention of being of service to someone, and you ask strategic questions and watch and listen, people will almost always tell you what they want, even if they don't realize they are doing it.

Social Competence Skill Supervisors Need: Ask Strategic and Timely Questions

There are eight different types of questions as indicated in the chart below[45]: Each might be used by supervisors for various reasons but generally, smart supervisors consistently apply a questioning strategy to achieve a specific end in mind or purpose.

There are five types of purpose. Everything, say on the job, should be for one of these four purposes.

Types of purpose:
- Give direction or request action.
- Get information (no immediate action required)
- Persuade
- Give an opinion, response or feedback
- Solve a problem

Type of question	Approach	Generally used for	Specific application for Manufacturing Supervisors
Closed "polar"	Invites a one-word answer, e.g., yes or	Easing into a communication or getting a quick	Give direction or request action, sometimes give information,

---

[45] Adapted from https://www.typetalk.com/blog/the-8-essential-questioning-techniques-you-need-to-know/

		no answer.	e.g., "Did you know X"
Open-ended	Cannot be answered with simple yes or no.	Encouraging wider discussion and elaboration, finding out more information.	Persuade and/or get information
Probing	A series of questions asked back to back, each subsequent question related to the answer giving to the prior question.	Gaining clarification and encouraging disclosure.	Get information and/or solve a problem
Leading	Coercive questions, sometimes presented more as a statement.	Leading a respondent towards a certain desired positive or negative route. (Can be perceived as manipulative)	Give direction and/or persuade but should be used carefully and not with intention to manipulate.
Loaded	Seem straightforward, closed questions but contain an assumption about the respondent.	Tricking a respondent into admitting a truth they would otherwise be willing to admit.	Should not be used
Funnel	Series of questions that begin broadly and then narrow, or begin narrowly and then broaden	Getting the maximum amount of information from someone. Sometimes used to diffuse tension or distract.	Get information and/or solve a problem

Recall and process	Require respondent to remember facts	Encourage critical thoughts and in-depth evaluation of a subject.	Give feedback and/or request direction
Rhetorical questions	Don't actually require an answer	Fostering agreement, persuasion, and/or a specific viewpoint.	Should not be used.

Supervisors need to learn what type of question is most appropriate in certain settings.

How Do You Teach Questioning Skills?

Generally speaking, as you experience different circumstances on the job, you learn to ask strategic questions. Strategic questions are questions devised for a specific purpose or to achieve a specific goal. A few examples:

HOW IS YOUR DAY QUESTION: When you want to assess a person's overall mood or address an attitudinal issue without overtly calling a person out on his/her behaviour, ask an open-ended how is your day? question such as:

a) How are you doing today, Bob?

b) Anything I can do for you, Pierre?

c) Hey Janet, you aren't your usual cheerful self, anything I can help with?

Responses might include:

a) I'd be fine if I could get some gloves. I have asked for them 3 times already, why can't I get any F7366&%!! gloves?

b) We are out of printer paper

c) Can you fix my paycheck?

These kinds of responses represent excellent opportunities to build trust and rapport. If people tell you what their issues are, get them what they need as quickly as you can. Don't say, "Ah, you have to speak to HR about your paycheck". Or, "refilling the paper in the copier is not my job".

Go get the gloves. Refill the copier paper, go to HR on behalf of the employee and try to resolve the payroll issue if you can. At that moment, why the person asked for gloves three times, or who he/she asked who didn't respond, who used the copier last, why the employee didn't record hours correctly, etc., none of this is relevant. The key thing is rewarding the person for answering the question and sharing information.

Show the person that you are humble, that you are not above doing small tasks, that he/she can trust you to do what you say you will do and most importantly, that you ask questions for a purpose and that you are listening to him/her. The person sees that you (as a supervisor/leader) won't ask them to do anything that you wouldn't do. They realize that you are doing tasks that you shouldn't have to do, but that you are a team player and you are helping them and that you are not selective- you help anyone, anytime you can. Your actions are job related but feel like a gesture of personal respect to the other person and this is a rapport builder.

WHAT WOULD HAPPEN IF QUESTION: When you need information to solve a problem but don't want to seem aggressive or parental, ask a what would happen if question such as:

a) So George, what would happen if we did x instead of y?

b) Betina, what do you think is the best way to get x done?

c) Hey Serge, I know in the past we did X, do you think there is a better way to do it?

Responses might include:

a) Well, if we do X, the temperature will increase and Y will happen, this is a problem because of Z

b) I would suggest we do X

c) Sure, I've been telling the day supervisor for 2 weeks that we should do X

The idea is that even if you know the answer to the question, but especially if you don't, the other person is given an opportunity to be an expert. He/she can share tribal knowledge or offer suggestions and feel like he/she is contributing to decision-making and/or valued for his/her expertise and contribution. The communication would continue with the supervisor asking more questions, e.g.,

a) Is there a way to do X without raising the temperature?

b) What could go wrong if we do X?

c) What do you think has prevented us from doing X in the past?

GET RIGHT TO THE POINT QUESTION: When you need to address a performance issue and don't have time to be indirect, ask a closed (yes or no) get right to the point question such as:

a) Viet, do you understand that you must wear safety goggles when you do x?

b) Inez, is it true you were smoking on the line?

c) So what you are telling me Darnel is that you have the tools you need to do Y, is that correct?

Responses might include:

a) Yes or No

b) Yes or No

c) Yes or no

The goal is to ask questions that require a yes or no response so that you can eliminate excuses one by one. If the response is a yes, you can close the communication with a directive, e.g.,

   a) Great, then I expect you will put your goggles on now and wear them every time you do task X.

   b) Okay, so you understand then that this is a breach of policy #01 and I have to write you up.

   c) Yes, you have the tools, perfect, so there is no reason you cannot complete the task, please do x by 1 pm.

If the responses are no, you continue the communication with an additional question.

   a) No, you didn't know that safety goggles are required? Okay so, did you complete the basic safety training as part of your onboarding program?

   b) So, you were not smoking on the line at 3 pm, as reported by person X? Can you explain why person X believed and reported that you were smoking?

   c) Okay, so you don't have the tools to do your job. What tools are you missing?

And you would continue to ask questions until you get positive responses.

Once you have the questioning part down, you will need to practice your listening skills. One listening strategy that I learned when I trained to be a Master Civility Trainer was to listen with TING.

Listening with TING is a bit different than the traditional active listening approach most of us have been taught. This because, TING incorporates aspects of civility which, as I ave suggested several times in this book, are frequently missing in how many supervisors communicate.

TING

EAR — MIND / EYE / HEART

Referencing the image above, the upper left part of the symbol stands for ear. We use our ear to hear the words the speaker is saying. The lower left-hand part of the symbol is for "king" or "dominant one", indicating that hearing the words through our ear is the most important part of the listening process.

In the upper right-hand part of the symbol, we see mind. Our minds help us understand the words the speaker is saying and the message they contain. Below that is eye. Our eyes allow us to see any non-verbal messages the speaker might be sending.

In the bottom right hand side is heart, and above that, the almost horizontal line translates to "one" or "to become of one[46]". Listening with heart is about pausing judgment and assuming the best of people, it means not rushing to conclusions and trying to remember the human condition as you listen. This heart part is new for most people and it takes practice to be able to truly listen in this way. As was mentioned earlier in the chapter, you don't want to go "deep" with people- that is, you don't ask or share very personal information, but as a listener, you try to remember that you are speaking to a person first, and a person doing a job second.

---

[46] https://leaderonomics.com/personal/better-leaders-listen-with-ting

You can show empathy and compassion, e.g., when someone is clearly upset, when there is injury, when others are emotional, but you work hard to manage your own emotions. Your team has to see you as someone who can be trusted to be calm, collected, and restrained under pressure.

Masotti Commonsense Social Competence Strategy #6 – Ask Strategic Questions

- ☐ See people as resources. Assume you can learn from them
- ☐ Be clear in your own mind about what exactly you need to know – what information are you seeking?
- ☐ Watch for the appropriate time to approach someone to ask questions e.g., don't bother employees right before lunch or during lunch or breaks. This is their personal time and they may resent your intrusion. Consider approaching at the end of the shift or just after a break or lunch
- ☐ Consider privacy and confidentiality
- ☐ Do not interrupt when the other person is talking
- ☐ Don't assume you already know the answer to the question you are asking
- ☐ Don't assume that the answer is correct or factual, be sure
- ☐ Don't assume that only one person has the answer or information you seek. Ask more than one person if possible
- ☐ Don't assume that one person speaks for the whole group
- ☐ Monitor your postures and nonverbal communication when listening e.g., avoid condescending or impatient gestures
- ☐ Listen with TING
- ☐ Ask a specific question, start with one question only. Avoid bombarding the person with many questions at once

- ☐ Chose a specific question for a specific purpose, e.g.,
    - ○ Ask a how is your day question to gauge morale or attitude
    - ○ Ask a get to the point question to hold someone accountable for a misbehaviour
    - ○ Ask a what would happen if question to get someone to share information or help resolve a problem
- ☐ Don't expect a thank you and don't say things like, "you owe me one", extend the gesture with no expectation of reciprocity

Please see Chapter 11 for Sources and Resources for ongoing learning.

Chapter 7
It Will Only Hurt for a Minute

"As a supervisor, you are going to have to look people in the eye and tell them the truth. You're going to have to discipline grown men and women, and some of them aren't going to like it. You are frequently not going to be the most popular guy in the room and occasionally your ego is going to take a punch. You're going to have to learn to bounce back and carry on."
- Christian Masotti

One of my all-time favorite quotes is by Mike Tyson who said, "everybody has a plan until they get punched in the mouth." In a 2012 interview with the former heavyweight champion, reporter Mike Berardino asked Tyson if he remembered the origins of that quote. Tyson responded, "people were asking me [before a fight], 'What's going to happen? They were talking about the other guy's style. He's going to give you a lot of lateral movement. He's going to move; he's going to dance. He's going to do this, do that, and I said, "Everybody has a plan until they get hit. Then, like a rat, they stop in fear and freeze.' " [47]

The reporter said that what he liked about the quote (and what I like about it too) is that its application stretches far beyond boxing. It really has meaning in any area of life. Most of us have a plan, but then we get punched in the face and the plan goes out the window. Whether the blow comes from a health issue, losing your job, making a bad investment, a traffic jam, whatever...it doesn't matter. It's how we react to that adversity that defines us, not the adversity itself. As a supervisor in manufacturing, I can tell you with experience that sometimes it feels like you are taking a beating daily. Between managers yelling at you, team members blind-siding you, people not showing up for work, people you thought had your back

---

[47] https://www.sun-sentinel.com/sports/fl-xpm-2012-11-09-sfl-mike-tyson-explains-one-of-his-most-famous-quotes-20121109-story.html

throwing you under the bus, constantly having to prove yourself and navigating tough interpersonal challenges daily, you can leave work pretty black and blue at the end of the day.

Not to say that this experience is acceptable, but the reality is, it's typical in a lot of manufacturing environments. I would imagine feeling like a human punching bag is familiar to supervisors in other sectors too. The point is, work can be hard, you're going to get punched, and most people can't take a punch. When things don't go according to plan, they freeze up. They are immobilized with fear or they don't have the ability to adapt and make a new plan. I find this to be true of many people in leadership positions. When things are going fine, no issues, no crisis, people showing up, job getting done, they seem to manage well. And they're happy to assume that the steady state is in large part due to some plan or action on their part. Some of the time they may be right about this. But it never fails that when the S%t#! hits the fan, these seemingly strong leaders fall apart.

Suddenly it was someone else's plan that failed. Suddenly the focus is on finding fault and making excuses. Some supervisors never come back from a bad situation. Maybe their team no longer trusts them, maybe they don't trust themselves, who knows. The reality is stuff happens. You must be able to bounce back. And the quicker you can do it the better.

Clearly, the hope is that you never have to take an actual physical punch to the face, but I guarantee you will take a few proverbial punches. Here are some examples:

- Being the brunt of "shop talk", e.g., backhanded comments as you walk by, being assigned an unfavorable nickname
- Being ignored
- Having people swear at you
- Having people gesture rudely directly at you

- Experiencing overt lying e.g., right to your face
- Experiencing sabotaging behaviour, e.g., people hiding your paperwork, etc.
- Having to listen to harsh feedback from your superiors
- Having to ask for help from people you have not established good relationships with
- Being passed over for promotions that are given to someone less committed or qualified
- Being disallowed from taking personal time, e.g., having to make hard choices between your personal and professional life
- Making significant errors and being called on them
- Having to admit you don't know something
- Having to apologize (for political reasons) for something you did not do
- Realizing that there will be no accolades or recognition for going the extra mile
- Being laid off or let go after years of loyal service
- Learning about untrue or unfair statements being made or negative impressions about you
- Having to defend your viewpoints and decisions constantly
- Being blamed ongoing for things that are not your responsibility

It is essential for supervisors to be resilient. Resilience is the ability to overcome hardship. In this case, we're talking about the mental aspects. The physical piece is "hardiness" and we discuss that in Chapter 9.

Being resilient means that you:

- ☐ Accept that you can't control everything but make effort to manage/control what you can
- ☐ See challenges and setbacks as opportunities to learn
- ☐ Focus on how you can avoid the set back in future

- Avoid blaming and finger-pointing
- Take responsibility for your own actions and responses
- Use coping strategies, e.g., manage your mindset (accept that setbacks are part of the process)
- Think before you act, e.g., to anticipate potential "punches"
- Try not to take things personally, e.g., whoever happened to be in the situation would have likely gotten punched, the punch probably wasn't directed at you specifically
- Take responsibility when you deserved the punch, e.g., you fell short of expectations, didn't do your due diligence, etc.
- Acknowledge that change is inevitable, and so accept it
- Try to remain positive
- Recognize that being in a leadership role means that you are not always going to be popular and so you focus on being trusted and respected instead

Basically, resilience is the ability to bounce back from or deal effectively with, adversity, adapt to sudden change, and to remain optimistic about life. Being resilient doesn't mean never experiencing mental stress or pain, it's about our ability to cope with emotional upheavals. Resilience is not something that we're born with – it develops over time as we acquire knowledge. A resilient workforce is one that performs well under pressure and deals quickly and effectively with change. Resilient employees don't dwell on failures or roadblocks. Instead, they move on and look to the future. They can deal with uncertainty and maintain their productivity and good humour despite the frustrations of everyday work life.[48]

What supervisor wouldn't prefer employees who respond to daily demands with enthusiasm and determination rather than fear, anger or resistance?

---

[48] Adapted from Leadership Toolkit, Workplace Education Manitoba, 2019

As a supervisor, you might not have control over adverse economic events or planned organizational changes, but you do have an important role to play in building a resilient team ready for whatever challenges come it's way. There are ways to facilitate resilience among your team members.

Key Take-Away

As a supervisor, you are going to have to look people in the eye and tell them the truth. You're going to have to discipline grown men and women, and some of them aren't going to like it. You are frequently not going to be the most popular guy in the room and occasionally your ego is going to take a punch. You're going to have to learn to bounce back and carry on.

Social Competence Skill Supervisors Need: Resilience

While it is true that some people are just born with natural mental stamina, most of us learn to be resilient through continuous learning and by experiencing success along with hardship. In workplace situations, as in sports, you can also teach mental toughness through discipline and by instilling habits that encourage a "we don't quit" attitude. It is this mental fortitude, which is the ability to focus, and refocus, and execute even when faced with roadblocks, uncertainty or adversity, that enables us to be resilient.

Low resilience can have serious consequences to an individual, to a team and to an organization. Supervisors should anticipate that in high-stress manufacturing environments where employees must deal with chronic change, it is easy for both supervisors and their team members to develop mental fatigue. As such you need to watch for the symptoms.

Emotional signs of mental exhaustion may include:

- Depression
- Anxiety

- Cynicism or pessimism
- Apathy (feeling of not caring)
- Detachment
- Anger
- Feelings of hopelessness
- Feeling of dread
- Lack of motivation
- Decline in productivity
- Difficulty concentrating

Physical signs of mental exhaustion may include:

- Headaches
- Upset stomach
- Body aches
- Chronic fatigue
- Changes in appetite
- Insomnia
- Weight gain or weight loss
- Increased illness, such as colds and flu

Behavioural Signs

Your mental exhaustion can cause you to behave in ways that are out of character for you. Behavioural signs may include:

- Poor performance at work
- Social withdrawal or isolation
- Inability to keep personal or work commitments
- Calling in sick to work or school more often[49]

As you might guess, having a team of resilient individuals can be a huge benefit to an organization. Building individual resilience is considered as one of three pillars for organizations to build adaptive capacity in times of change. The World Economic Forum declares,

---

[49] https://www.healthline.com/health/mental-exhaustion#symptoms

Individuals' mindset and efforts will be key… for people to become creative, curious, agile lifelong learners, comfortable with continuous change." This ideal mindset requires resilience. We often think of resilience as a personality trait, but in fact, it can be learned. Resilience is comprised of seven factors, or competencies, which increase and enable self-management, self-awareness, realistic optimism, empathy and reaching out to connect with others. With resilience training, employees regard the unknown from a different point of view, moving from "what will I lose?" to "whatever happens, I'll be okay." In the face of change, resilience creates a growth mindset.

The second pillar for building adaptive capacity is to create a network of empowered and agile teams. As employees grow in resilience, so teams acquire the strength to adapt quickly, and this quality is implicit in agile teams. Invented to cope with the need for continuous change, agile teams stress clarity of mission and focus, accountability, flexible thinking and problem solving, mutual trust and psychological safety. A resilient team is skilled in managing change, including changes in its membership, makeup, and authority. Without such resilience, team productivity would break under the pressure of change.

Leaders of empowered teams also must change to act as coaches and mentors, not hands-on micromanagers. This leadership integrity is the third pillar for building adaptive and resilient organizations. This is a dramatic break from the top-down structure that has defined organizations for generations, and candid leadership will admit to its own need for resilience when taking on this transformation.

Every new normal tests an organization's culture. Like individuals and teams, culture is stressed by changing circumstances. No single person "owns" a culture, but as a leader, you embody and exhibit the values that underlie culture. Will they change in times of disruption?

Leadership's answer to this question has a major impact on the resilience of the workplace itself. meQuilibrium researched the values of hundreds of organizations over the last seven years, including Fortune 500 companies and government departments. We've discovered that organizational resilience requires putting stated values into action—in other words, integrity.

Integrity builds trust across the board, in good times and tough times. You cannot guarantee the future—and employees know that—but you can assure employees that, whatever happens, you will act according to the values they know and share.[50]

How Do You Teach Resilience?

Psychologist Sherry Campbell suggests there are 8 ways to build mental fortitude[51]

1. Define your win
Winning should never mean taking the easy way out. Winning is all about competing with the challenge at hand and coming out with the result we want. To be smart and execute well, we must examine the holes in our plan that our challenge has revealed to us and find the most efficient ways to build a plan that will fill those gaps.

2. Create efficient procedures
When we are in the eye of the storm of any adversity,

---

[50] https://www.forbes.com/sites/janbruce/2018/09/05/change-is-the-new-normal-how-will-you-handle-it/#219741243959

[51] https://www.entrepreneur.com/article/311791

we must hold our emotional reactions enough to be able to utilize the mental objectivity we need to establish the procedures and strategies necessary to attain our goals. Failure is sometimes the exact thing we need to experience in order to know what procedures, structures or strategies are missing. The more efficient our foundational procedures are, the easier it is to remain mentally tough because it is the stability of our procedures that give us something to count on.

3. Set priorities
It's hard to possess the mental fortitude necessary to succeed when we lack organization at the base of our business structure. If we don't prioritize our critical stressors to come first, we act as our own roadblock to success. When fear or failure are present it is too easy to focus on the non-critical details that don't matter but convince us we're making progress.

4. Self-evaluation
Mental fortitude means we must operate with honesty and integrity. We must take ownership for what is not working properly, whether that is us or something else in our business model. Mentally tough people are not afraid to look in the mirror every day and examine where they have room to improve. To perform well doesn't require perfection as much as it requires the humility to know what is and is not achievable in the moment.

5. Self-control
If we want to succeed on any level, we cannot be weak to our more reactive emotions. We must learn to manage the degree to which we are always on the edge of losing our mental fortitude to emotions such as fear, anger, frustration or even excitement. When we are effective in managing our emotions, we better

prepare ourselves to function at our peak performance levels.

6. Prepare for negotiations
To have the mental fortitude and stability we need to be successful, it is wise to prepare ourselves to have the answers we need. When we create the proper communication scripts, we are more confident in meetings and prepared with the intelligent answers to the top questions we will be asked by potential new opportunities.

7. Mental training
The more we use our mind, the more we stretch and challenge it, the stronger it gets. It is important to set up a daily mental workout to dramatically improve our focus, so we can execute with consistency. We need to practice self-examination, goal-setting, and problem-solving.

8. Relentless optimism.
Success is not built upon negative thinking. To have the mental fortitude necessary to achieve on any level, we must work to replace our pessimistic thinking with hopeful thinking. Attitude is everything. With a relentlessly positive and open mindset, we are better disciplined to complete the tasks necessary to make our solutions materialize.[52]

In addition to the above, I have found it useful to incorporate pre-emptive rituals and habits into my daily work routine. What I mean by this is that I try to anticipate and plan for potential punches and manage them before they happen. For example, manufacturing organizations typically capture a lot of data. If you understand the kinds of issues that frequently arise, you can use the data to manage them.

---

[52] https://www.entrepreneur.com/article/311791

Let's say that scheduling and manpower are ongoing issues. You are constantly getting punched in the face when people don't show up for work. If you review the data you can often identify patterns in absenteeism e.g., Joe seems to call in sick on Mondays. Now that you know this, you can change Joe's schedule to accommodate this unplanned day off, or you can schedule a back up anticipating that Joe will simply not show up. If you are having to deal with equipment breakdowns, check the maintenance records and implement more frequent maintenance or order parts you need in advance due to anticipating needing to update or change out a part. If you review corrective action reports and personnel files, you can sometimes also see patterns in collaboration or productivity related to when certain people are scheduled together and you can manage that potential punch by adjusting things – the idea is to pick out what you can control. You might be surprised at how much you can manage.

Another strategy I have found useful is to be mindful of how you label things, e.g., if I see someone being late as a sign of disrespect directed towards me, and I feel that behaviour as a punch, I'm going to react a certain way. But if I instead see the behaviour as a skills gap that I can address, e.g., the employee needs some coaching in time management, then I approach the situation as a normal part of my job which is to solve people problems. It is no longer a punch.

Masotti Commonsense Social Competence Strategy #7 – Build Resilience (Learn to take a punch)
- ☐ Show people how the work they do is valued on the job, e.g., why is enduring the hardship worth it?
- ☐ Make people aware of the type of challenges they may face on the job
- ☐ Provide opportunities for people to see how others managed those challenges in the past
- ☐ Build your own resilience, e.g., model resilient behaviour for example:
    - ○ Have a positive attitude

- Name your fears, and face them
- Set small achievable personal goals ongoing so that you can experience success
- Encourage others, e.g., foster optimism
- Don't take yourself too seriously, e.g., have a sense of humor
- Take advantage of social supports around you, e.g., ask for help when you need it
- Encourage autonomy
- Provide opportunities to practice coping strategies
- Build "time out" opportunities into daily routine, e.g., make sure people get breaks
- Incorporate positive language, e.g., affirmations, into workplace slogans and mottos
- Provide team supports, e.g., buddy and mentor programs

Please see Chapter 11 for Sources and Resources for ongoing learning.

Chapter 8
Actually, I Know Absolutely Nothing About Trains

> *"It does not matter how much you think you know,* ***"collaboration is currency in the new world of work"****. An essential aspect of supervising is collaboration, and to be a good collaborator you need to consistently and consciously exhibit civility. I have learned that Civility is a continuous improvement strategy for building strong interpersonal relationships at work."* – Christian Masotti

August 2017, I interviewed for a position with Bombardier. I had applied for the position of Production Supervisor for planes with the company previously and so had just assumed that the interview was for that same position. It became apparent that I was actually being interviewed for a position as a Maintenance Supervisor for trains when one of the interviewers asked me directly what kind of experience I had with trains. What could I do except be honest? I told the interviewers "Actually, I know nothing about trains. But I do know:

- How to build trust
- How to engage others in continuous improvement
- How to communicate in a respectful way
- How to give feedback
- How to evaluate performance
- How unions work
- How to collect metrics
- How to evaluate data
- How to take directions
- How to manage time and resources
- How to make effective decisions
- And…I had 20 years of experience in automotive and surely some of that would be transferable.

And, what do you know, I got the job!

Admittedly, the first few weeks in the position, I had to overcome a grueling learning curve. But in the end, all of the other skills I had acquired over the years enabled me to be successful on the job. I would say that one essential strategy that helped me achieve success was the ability to interact well with others and to build trust such that they wanted to work with me. Specifically, I have learned how to collaborate.

This ability to foster collaboration takes time to learn. Collaboration is different from teamwork. In my experience, "collaboration" is specifically about problem-solving with a group of people who have different skills and experience. For example, I had to be able to supervise and direct activities of people who knew how to fix trains, but I knew nothing about trains. In addition, my mindset (as a supervisor) and the way I think, what my priorities and habits are, was also different from the people I was working with.

The "team" – which I would describe as a work group with similar interests, skill sets, and goals, were engaging in teamwork. They were working concurrently with me and with their work team to meet their daily targets and achieve their goals. In theory, I was part of the team, but when there are designated roles and responsibilities as well as designated leadership i.e., me as a supervisor, the dynamics of the activity are different. People communicate and act differently. I assess this difference as due to unequal power among the team members.

With collaboration, there can't be any assigned leaders. Everyone has to feel equal. The group self-directs. If they do designate roles they do so as a collective, e.g., vote someone in, roles are not assigned. Each member of the group is understood to contribute something, and the contribution could be entirely different than what other team members contribute. In addition, with collaboration, the focus is usually on problem solving. At least that has been my experience anyway.

In manufacturing, for example, the production team might interact and communicate, they brainstorm, they discuss things, but at the end of the day no one on that team can make a decision, that is the responsibility of the supervisor.

So, as you can imagine, I was in a totally new environment, I knew nothing about trains, but in order for me to be able to do my job, I had to get information from people who knew more than me about the equipment and the schedules and the day to day operations. As a supervisor in training, I had to build rapport and trust so that they could participate in the decision-making until I got my bearings. I had to be a part of the team.

In many cases in the early months on that job, I would essentially be asking the production team member who I was supervising what the best course of action was. Basically, he/she made the decision. Then I would consider my boss's priorities, assess big picture impacts, e.g., to the next shift, the organization overall, to suppliers, etc., and agree or disagree.

If I had not been able to become part of the team, there is no way I could have learned what I needed to learn in a short time, and there is no way I would have been successful in that position. What I came to understand is that when you are training, you have a huge opportunity to make things easier on yourself. During the training period, expectations are relatively low, e.g., you aren't expected to make significant changes or improvements. It is during the training period when you have all the supports you need, right there in front of you, and no accountability except to learn. It's during the training period where the hierarchy is flattened for a short time and you are perceived as one of the team, this makes collaboration possible. Embrace that time. It's a tremendous gift.

Over the years, I have seen many times where collaboration is critical to problem-solving. The challenge is that many supervisors do not have the humility or civility to enable them to collaborate effectively.

Key Take-Away

If you are not the most experienced or the most educated person, you had better be humble enough to acknowledge this fact. And, you had better be open to learning ongoing, and to learning from others. It does not matter how much you think you know, *"**collaboration is currency in the new world of work**"*[53].

Social Competence Skill Supervisors Need: Collaboration

An essential aspect of supervising is collaboration, and to be a good collaborator you need to consistently and consciously exhibit civility. I have learned that **civility is a continuous improvement strategy for building strong interpersonal relationships at work.** Civility, for those who may not know, is an aspect of character. Being nice is part of it, we discussed this in Chapter 2, but it's more about how you treat people generally- how you make people feel. If you can learn how to show people though how you speak and interact with them that you value them, it is incredible how willing people will be to collaborate with you.

However, if you are unkind to people, if you are self-focused, ego-oriented, and uncivil such that people do not perceive you as trustworthy or credible, the likelihood that they will do anything more than the absolute minimum required to support you is very low.

In my experience, character can take you farther than competence. Civility is a point of character and it is civility that frequently differentiates average leaders from great leaders. When you adopt civility as a core value you have a distinct advantage when collaboration is required because:

---

[53] Dr. Lewena Bayer, *The 30percent Solution*, Motivational Press, 2016

- You have been treating people well all along and so they trust you e.g., they don't think you are pretending to be equal in a collaboration situation
- You have presented yourself as humble enough to ask for help.
- You have set your ego aside and helped a team member where possible, e.g., you have shown that you are not above doing production tasks.
- You have shown people that you see each member of the team as having value, in this way people know you will not favor or buddy up with one person on the team.
- You are consistently direct and transparent, so people know your true intention is problem-solving versus trying to ingratiate yourself.
- You are calm. You don't yell you don't bully others. As such people feel safe disagreeing with you – and this is necessary for true collaboration.

Frequently we don't know what we don't know- until we are in a setting where we have to draw on our personal resources. Navigating these situations is about taking measured risks, being willing to learn, and understanding that everything you do builds skills- even if you don't quite know how you will use them at the time you are learning them. It's also key to remember that you have a very specific and unique experience and skillset, relative to the people you are working with. And each of those people also has something potentially new or useful to offer. That you can exchange information or leverage each other's skills so that every one of you doesn't have to know everything is incredibly valuable. In addition, having a range of thinking styles and mindsets in the room can help drive creativity and innovation.

In addition to adopting civility as a core value and striving to exhibit it daily, I have found the following strategies are also useful when you want to foster collaboration:

a) Take inventory of your own skills and experience. In doing so, you discover (and can label) all kinds of bits of knowledge, experience, and lessons learned that you could offer up to someone else. In addition, you can identify skill or experiential areas where you may need to draw on others as a resource. When you do this inventory, keep the following in mind:
   i. Don't audit yourself. Log everything, event short projects or jobs you'd like to forget. Make a list of all the tasks and responsibilities you had at those jobs.
   ii. Where possible, try to include specific achievements, e.g., don't just say you know how to do spreadsheets, record the kind of information you put into spreadsheets, the software you used, etc.
   iii. Include volunteer and other unpaid work as well, e.g., if you have been managing the finances at the community center or coaching Peewee Hockey for ten years, that is valuable experience.
   iv. Include skills that relate to your hobbies, e.g., if you are an avid rock climber you may have knowledge about terrain or geography or some other niche expertise that could be valuable to someone else. In addition, your hobbies can tell people a lot about your personality, how you take risks, how extroverted you are, etc.
   v. Include all types of education, e.g., if you attended pilot training sessions, took a free course, etc., that knowledge is still potentially useful.
   vi. Be as specific as possible. E.g., instead of listing, "outdoor activities" state the specific activities such as hiking, running, skiing. Instead of saying you are a

member of Continuous Improvement Committee at work, list what you actually do, e.g., you are the Membership Coordinator. The more specific you are the better.
b) Devise a skill matrix showing all the various skills and abilities of every member of your team. Post it somewhere where everyone can see it. Not only does doing this show the team who has what skill, but it can also be an incentive for people to gain additional skills, and it helps the team understand why it is beneficial to work together.

How Do You Teach Collaboration?

The key to teaching collaboration is creating a workplace culture that encourages meaningful exchange between people. If the culture has well-ingrained silos or there is high mistrust, this isn't going to be an easy task.
performance. People have to feel valued and they have to feel safe.

You have to consider each person's strengths and sometimes what motivates him/her. You also have to balance autonomy and collaboration, for example, you don't want to create an environment where people cannot work independently e.g., due to strong reliance on the team.

A Stanford study found that people working collaboratively stuck at their task for 64 percent longer than those working individually on the same task. It also reported higher levels of engagement and success and lower levels of fatigue[54]. In my experience, it makes good sense to deliberately create scenarios that require collaboration.

---

[54]

https://www.sciencedirect.com/science/article/abs/pii/S0022103114000420?viapercent3Dihub

Again, this is different from teamwork where for example, each person is doing his specific part to achieve a known common goal. With collaboration, you know there is a problem that needs to be solved, but you don't know what the solution or endpoint is, and you don't know exactly how you will get there.

So, recognizing that collaboration is good for individuals, the team, and for the company, why don't organizations teach it or encourage it more? The challenge is that people collaborating must possess excellent interpersonal skills as it's very important that every person involved contributes their ideas, opinions, and knowledge[55]. As such, to teach collaboration you have to teach civility. Civility incorporates aspects of:

- **Social Intelligence** – includes reading verbal, nonverbal, and contextual cues. Supports communication, builds trust and empathy, and fosters presence.
- **Cultural Competence** – includes demographic and organizational culture. Supports communication, builds trust, humility, gratitude, and compassion, and fosters respect and collaboration.
- **Systems Thinking** – includes understanding the impact of one's role, one's place in terms of contribution to the larger picture, internal and external influences, etc. Fosters change readiness, adaptive capacity, problem-solving and builds engagement.
- Continuous Learning – includes learning how to learn, learning from mistakes, assessing risk, learning from others. Fosters self-control, autonomy, change-readiness, solutions mindset and confidence.

---

[55] https://www.civilservicecollege.org.uk/news-understanding-the-differences-between-teamwork-and-collaboration-203

Dr. Janice Presser, a behavioural scientist and Co-Founder and CEO, **The Gabriel Institute** and **Teamability.com** suggests that "people like best what they do best, and they do best what they like best," says Dr. Presser. Keys to developing team collaboration are:

- Align each person's job responsibilities (at least in part) with the specific kind of team contribution that person will find meaningful.
- Determine the modes of teaming that are most-needed for a particular team's mission, and make sure that they are represented on the team.

Here is some helpful terminology:

- **Role:** A person's affinity for one or more specific modes of service to the needs of a team.
- **Coherence:** Expressed as positive, flexible, constructive teaming behaviours under varying conditions of stress and ambiguity.
- **Teaming Characteristics:** Individual styles of responding and relating to others; subject to situational context. Understand and apply the following Elements of Team Operation (easily learned ways to communicate in alignment with a person's mode of contribution):
1. **Role-fit:** An appropriate match between a person's role and their assigned set of job responsibilities, raising individual performance and engagement.
2. **Team-fit:** Structuring a team to include the roles that are best-fit to the team's mission, to optimize overall team performance.
3. **Role-pairing:** Known, replicable synergies between specific roles, which improve resilience and team chemistry.
4. **Role-respect:** The unique manner in which people of different roles experience appreciation and respect, used in management to build trust and team stability.

Dr. Presser continues, "The most important thing to have when developing a collaborative culture is a clear understanding of teaming needs and challenges, and the most important thing(s) to look for are the teaming qualities that will ensure success under those working conditions. To build positive, collaborative team interaction it is essential to recognize that a team has a life of its own, and that different modes of teaming can be just as important to collaboration and productivity as different areas of expertise are to the work that needs to be done."[56]

For details about how to teach civility including how to incorporate it into your performance evaluations, daily feedback, onboarding, etc., please review "*Lean on Civility*" Masotti & Bayer, 2020, which includes expanded content and practical tools.

Masotti Commonsense Social Competence Strategy #8 – Foster Collaboration

- ☐ Be approachable
- ☐ Don't take yourself too seriously
- ☐ Be able to say "I don't know"
- ☐ Be transparent
- ☐ Assume there are people in the room smarter than you are
- ☐ Acknowledge the experience, skills, and credentials of others
- ☐ Be curious, ask questions
- ☐ Ask for help
- ☐ Take notes, show that you are serious about the information you are seeking
- ☐ Review the process that supports collaboration
- ☐ Offer support, with no strings attached

---

[56] https://www.smartsheet.com/collaborative-teamwork

- ☐ Be honest about what you know
- ☐ Share what you know
- ☐ Stick to the facts when you can, avoid opinion
- ☐ Thank others who share with you
- ☐ Credit others with information they share with you that you pass on
- ☐ Strive to exceed expectations, e.g., give more than is required
- ☐ Implement a process to ensure that all collaborators have an opportunity to share
- ☐ Set ground rules for communication in collaboration settings
- ☐ Invite varied opinions and discussion – disagreement is sometimes a good thing
- ☐ Encourage wild ideas, creativity, and innovation
- ☐ Create a psychologically safe environment where others feel free to speak
- ☐ Maintain confidentiality where applicable

"If you are not the most experienced or the most educated person, you had better be humble enough to acknowledge this fact. And, you had better be open to learning ongoing, and to learning from others" – Christian Masotti

Please see Chapter 11 for Sources and Resources for ongoing learning.

Chapter 9
Be a Strong Competitor

"Sometimes work is tough. Sometimes people are going to disappoint you, and sometimes your work and even your life will suck. But you're going to have to figure out, no one is going to hold your hand. Put your work boots on, make sure your radio charged, be a grown-up, and get on with the day" - Christian Masotti

Okay, I get that we are all human. And sometimes life (and work specifically) totally sucks. Between being laid off a few times, fired a few times, the growing pains in between and all the eating S%4!x I had to do when I first started out, I might even say that work sucks *most* of the time, people will disappoint you *much* of the time, and it generally sucks to have to work *all* of the time. But, but if you focus on the reasons you're working and think about the long-term benefits, or pay attention to what you learn along the way, it does get easier to get up and go to work every day.

When I was a kid, my uncle Fernand St. Germain told me that "success is easy, all it takes is hard work" he was top salesman for Canada every year in his sales job due to building relationships with his customers. I had an opportunity to see him at work for a short time and learned that it's not easy committing to showing up every day, doing your very best, and being happy about the job you do. It takes discipline. It takes practice. It takes fine tuning your routines and processes so that you can achieve everything you need to achieve.

For most people it takes resilience and mental toughness to face the world every day, and some also need courage to make difficult decisions that impact others. Occasionally, it also takes sacrifice, e.g., sometimes you have to work weekends or overtime, etc. All of this is true for supervisors in manufacturing. You definitely need to be resilient (mentally strong).

I have found, however, that mental toughness, that is, having the will or desire to succeed, and being able to bounce back from psychological hardship isn't always enough, especially in manufacturing. Because of the harsh conditions in manufacturing, you also have to be "hardy".

Hardiness is about physical strength. It's about stamina. It's about being a grown-up and possessing the stereotypical "toughness" that is often associated with masculinity. It's about having a little fight in you, being a competitor. (For the record, I believe women can be tough too, this quality is often just expressed in a different way).

Me, personally, I've always been a competitor. I liked doing better than the next guy, I liked outdoing myself. I had a short stint in professional football for the Canadian Football League and I learned exactly how you need both resilience and hardiness to succeed. I'm also a problem-solver. I like fixing things and so what might seem like a challenge to others, feels like a learning opportunity to me. If you like to problem-solve, you don't get bored in manufacturing– there is always another problem to solve. Being able to fix things, to fine-tune processes, to figure something out or to learn a skill you didn't know before has always been a confidence booster for me. It's a mindset really. No question over the years, the mental game has been a strain at times, and when things got really tough, I believe it was my hardiness that got me through. My experience has been that hardiness is a useful social competence strategy in that when you exhibit hardiness, others see you as confident, disciplined, goal-oriented, strong, reliable, credible, and focused. This is exactly the kind of impression a supervisor wants to convey.

I can't remember when exactly, but I remember reading a story about SS Navy Seal, Jesse Goggins who is the only member of the United States Armed Forces to complete SEAL training, United States Army Ranger School, *and* Air Force Tactical Air Controller training.

In the article, there was a reference to research stating that it is a fact that when you think you have had enough e.g., in terms of what you can withstand physically, you really have the capacity for up to 60 percent more output. This information has helped me adopt hardiness as a social competence strategy because I am now able to tell myself that when I think I am tired I really have the capacity to do 60 percent more. And although I try not to push too hard, I also know that when it comes down to crunch time, my team also has the capacity to do more than they think. When I show I believe in them in this way, they usually come through for me. There is a supporting article in *The Hustle* referencing this 40 percent Rule and how it is a secret for Navy Seals' mental toughness.[57] This rule a proven scientific mental framework that can help you push yourself beyond your limits.

Key Take-Away:

Sometimes work is tough. Sometimes people are going to disappoint you, and sometimes your work (and even your life) will suck. But you're going to have to figure out, no one is going to hold your hand. Find out what makes you feel confident and strong. Put your work boots on, make sure your radio charged, be a grown-up, and get on with the day.

Social Competence Skill Supervisors Need: Hardiness

In my experience, there are three aspects to hardiness, they are:

- Physicality (your physical strength and stamina)
- Confidence (being able to claim and use your strengths)
- Self-direction (being able to figure out what you need to be successful and doing whatever that is)

From a practical point of view, one might not know that he/she will require hardiness until a specific social, personal, or work

---

[57] https://thehustle.co/40-percent-rule-navy-seal-secret-mental-toughness

situation creates stress that he/she is not accustomed to dealing with. Initially, it is the following skills that enable a person to be hardier:

- Be present e.g., pay attention to what is going on around you. If you notice gradual changes and adjust ongoing, adapting is easier than if you have not paid attention and suddenly find yourself faced with significant challenge or change.
- Admit when you are over your head. Do some personal reflection. Take note of your limitations. When faced with a situation that you feel you can't handle, ask for help.
- See the change as a learning opportunity. Rather than perceive yourself as a victim that is being done to- and has no control, see yourself as having the opportunity to make choices about how to move forward. Take the opportunity to learn.
- Manage your physicality. Eat healthy foods, get some exercise, take some wind downtime. Be aware of your "constitution". With reference to health, constitution means the physical makeup of a person. ... If you have a strong constitution, it means you don't get sick very often.[58]

The fact is, while you might be lucky enough to have a mentor who offers some tips for surviving the workplace, most of us have to go it alone. No one holds your hand. No one is going to baby you or go overboard to make sure you are okay every day. It's up to you to sort that out. Figure out what makes you feel good and healthy, and confident, and strong, and do those things.

My experience has been that most manufacturing workplaces strive to standardize jobs. There are controls in place so that a 21-year-old football player can do the job, and/or a 65-year-old

---

[58] https://www.quora.com/What-does-it-mean-to-have-a-weak-constitution

woman can also do the job. Anyone should be able to succeed.

Knowing this, I have also learned is that when grownups at work make issue about little things that they should be managing themselves, or can't do the job for some reason, it's either a skills issue, e.g., an attempt to distract from incompetence, or it's a cry for attention, which I perceive as a hardiness issue. In either case, it's not very mature and if you indulge these behaviours, you are encouraging social dependence and unprofessionalism. Some real-life examples of low hardiness are when you observe employees:

- ☐ Feigning injury because he/she needs attention for some reason
- ☐ Asking for extra time on breaks to manage some personal issue that is not your concern
- ☐ Deliberately working slowly to make a point or draw attention
- ☐ Purposefully not following process because he/she wasn't consulted about some change or situation
- ☐ Being unnecessarily loud or aggressive as a show of personal power or defiance

On the job, being hardy is indicated by behaviour such as:

- ☐ Avoiding complaining about a small injury
- ☐ Showing up, ready for work, regardless of whether you feel like it or not
- ☐ Working through manageable illnesses, e.g., you wouldn't go home because you have the sniffles
- ☐ Resisting complaining or whining when things are not easy
- ☐ Avoiding taking short cuts e.g., that might impact others in a negative way
- ☐ Taking on extra work if it benefits you, your family or the team
- ☐ Finishing the work, e.g., not leaving until the job is done
- ☐ Pulling your weight- literally, e.g., not leaving the dirty

- or hard jobs to someone else
- ☐ Taking time to rest when necessary and possible
- ☐ Taking care of your own personal needs, e.g., bring a lunch
- ☐ Having the ability to manage your own stress
- ☐ Working through physical pain, e.g., go see the nurse after the shift
- ☐ Taking necessary precautions to protect oneself, e.g., wearing safety gear
- ☐ Taking turns, e.g., to alleviate hardship for someone else
- ☐ Figuring out your own messes, e.g., you don't have to share all your personal issues and traumas
- ☐ Taking calculated risks
- ☐ Being strong enough to admit when you make a mistake
- ☐ Asking for help, but not as a means of doing less, just asking when you really need the help
- ☐ Being confident in your abilities
- ☐ Squaring up with others directly, e.g., if you have a problem with someone go talk to him/her
- ☐ Taking care of your health, e.g., eat, sleep, exercise, do what you have to do to feel good
- ☐ Trying new things, e.g., experiment with wellness habits that might benefit you
- ☐ Being energized or excited about new challenges
- ☐ Being open and ready for change

How Do You Teach Hardiness?

For the most part, I believe that learning to be hardy a something each individual has to take on for him/herself. I don't feel it's the employer or organization's responsibility to train employees in this area.

Aside from working to ensure safety, I think each of, as adults at work, we should be able to take care of ourselves.

However, Psychologist Dr. Salvatore Maddi claims there are 3 C's of hardiness. These are challenge, control, and commitment. Maddi suggests that if you can teach these key characteristics of successful coping, people will flourish through hard times.

> **Challenge is the first C of hardiness.** How we view a problem is important. Hardy individuals see problems as challenges rather than threats. This difference is important because when faced with a threat, there is a tendency to try and avoid it. Hardy people see problems as challenges and rather than being overwhelmed and seeking to retreat, they get busy looking for solutions. Seeing a problem as a challenge mobilizes our resources to deal with it and encourages us to pursue the possibilities of a successful outcome.
>
> **The second C of hardiness is control.** In a tough situation, hardy individuals do not become overwhelmed or helpless. Instead, they strive to gain control of what they can by going into action. While acknowledging it is true that many aspects of a crisis situation cannot be controlled, they also understand that by intentionally developing and holding onto a positive, optimistic, hopeful outlook, we can always determine our reaction to any predicament we face. We can choose our best attitude, and the better we are at doing this, the greater our sense of being in charge of our circumstances.
>
> **Commitment is the third C of hardiness.** It refers to persevering or sticking it out through a hard time. Being committed to an outcome keeps us going even in the midst of setbacks, obstacles, and discouraging news. Being committed to a goal helps us overcome occasional losses of motivation and remain steadfast in our efforts.[59]

---

[59] http://www.lessons4living.com/wmaz_week196.htm

In terms of day-to-day hardiness, I have found that you just have to make a process that works for you and enables you to deal with whatever strenuous thing you are having to manage. For example, I work long days. Sometimes I work 12 hours at one job and go straight to another job. Over time, I have developed a process for managing this and as a result, built up my level of hardiness such that now working 36 or even 48 hours straight is manageable for me. (I don't recommend it, but I have done it and managed it)

Masotti Method for Managing Long Workdays

- Keep your eye on the prize, e.g., remind yourself why you are working the extra shift or the long hours
- Stay busy; if the work tasks aren't filling the time, read a newspaper, listen to a podcast, take an online course related to the work, review workplace materials, just keep busy.
- Stay hydrated; 14 cups of coffee and 6 donuts is maybe not the best idea, but maybe a cup of coffee will give you a boost. And drink lots of water.
- Stand up, when you start to feel sleepy, stand up. It's much harder to sleep standing up.
- Cool off- literally. Go stand in front of a fan, open a window, take a short walk outside if it's cooler.
- Take a cat nap- if allowable and at the appropriate time and place. Set the alarm on your phone and find a quiet corner- even 15 minutes can give you the boost you need to get up and finish what you need to do.

Whether your organization teaches it, or you have to take on learning to be hardy yourself, the benefits of being hardy include:

- Fewer sick days
- Increased stamina, e.g., you can sustain longer work periods

- Decreased boredom
- Increased opportunity to learn new things
- Balanced personality, e.g., hardy people tend to be resilient and positive
- Longer, healthier life
- Increased exposure to high performing people, e.g., like attracts like
- Frequent experiences of success
- Increased respect of others, e.g., admiration for discipline, longevity, perseverance

Masotti Commonsense Social Competence Strategy #9– Be Hardy

- ☐ Anticipate and plan for a physically demanding environment, e.g., consider what you and/or your team needs to work well related to:
    - Noise
    - Deadlines
    - Moving equipment
    - Moving vehicles
    - Ventilation: quality and noise associated with
    - Repetitive motion
    - Safety equipment e.g., that hinders movement
    - Physical barriers to communication
    - Tight spaces
    - Large, open spaces
    - Difficulty related to equipment
    - Range of motion required
    - Time standing
    - Distance to areas you need to go to on the job, e.g., parking lot to work site
    - Availability of washrooms
    - Allowable breaks
    - Allergens
    - Chemicals
    - General morale
    - Temperature in the room
    - Availability of food and water

- ○ Availability of first aid or emergency equipment
- ☐ Take care of your personal needs:
    - ○ Sleep when you can and for a reasonable amount of time
    - ○ Keep up with regular body maintenance: dentist, eye doctor, doctor
    - ○ Have a supply of any required medications on hand
    - ○ Exercise regularly
    - ○ Eat a healthy diet
    - ○ Practice effective stress management
    - ○ Practice good hygiene, e.g., hair, nails, shaving, etc.
    - ○ Make it a habit to keep clothes clean and in good repair
    - ○ Maintain safety standards, e.g., wear safety equipment
- ☐ Watch for typical "look and behaviour" when you/or others are doing the job. If there is variance, or off-standard look and behaviour, consider if that behaviour is impacting performance. If it is, you need to address what you are seeing.
    - ○ You don't need to know the reason, you just identify and call out the behaviour e.g., to prevent an injury, etc.
    - ○ Observe and ask questions to discover the cause of the off-standard behaviour, e.g., is it due to:
        - ☐ Drugs
        - ☐ Alcohol
        - ☐ Nervous breakdown
        - ☐ High stress
        - ☐ External situation, e.g., personal trauma
        - ☐ Illness
        - ☐ Depression
        - ☐ Hunger
        - ☐ Exhaustion
        - ☐ Distress

Please see Chapter 11 for Sources and Resources for ongoing learning.

Chapter 10
You Are Exactly Where You Want To Be

"It does not matter what people say. People say all kinds of things for all kinds of reasons and you can't put a lot of stock into words. However, **how a person acts, usually tells you what he/she really thinks***, what his/her goals and values are, and who he/she is as a person. We each have the power to make choices and devise a life we are proud of. Where we are at any given time is a reflection of our choices."* – Christian Masotti

If I had a nickel for every time I heard:
- Someone who has been on the job for years says (day in and day out) *"I'm going quit this stupid job."*
- Someone who can't even manage to be on time for work, say, *"I could do a better job managing this team than X does"*
- Someone who complains every time I see him/her about not having enough money, say, *"Yeah, I spent $200 at the bar last night"* or *"I really don't want to work the overtime"*.
- Someone who just took a bit of his/her 3rd donut says, *"I am going to lose 10 pounds."*

And so on…. I'd be rich!

Over the years I have learned that people who talk a lot about doing something are rarely the people who actually do things. People who have a plan, work the plan. They don't talk nonstop about what they are going to do. They don't need constant advice and fluffing up, or feedback. They don't sit around and complain. They make a decision, and then they get busy getting whatever it is they need to get done.

Similarly, what you say isn't always a true reflection of who you are. For example, you can take on the role of supervisor and tell me you are a "people person" or that you value people. And then when I ask how much time you spend on the production floor speaking to people during your shift, you can't say- because you spend most of your time at work in the office. It doesn't make any sense. I have learned that how people spend their time is usually a good reflection of what they truly value and what their personal values are.

In terms of the reality of work, I understand that people talk about what they imagine doing or wish they could do, etc., as a way of coping with circumstances they feel they have no control over. Sadly, a whopping 80 percent of Americans state being dissatisfied with their jobs[60]. People aren't happy at work and so they talk about whatever they think might make them happy. But talking isn't the same as taking action. It's just talking.

I don't find it surprising that the *Mind the Workplace Report*, released by the nonprofit group Mental Health America (MHA) and The Faas Foundation, which surveyed more than 17,000 workers in 19 industries found that 71 percent were either "actively looking for new job opportunities" or had the topic on their minds "always, often or sometimes" at work. Only 19 percent said they "rarely or never" think about getting a new job[61].

Most days, it's pretty clear to me that the majority of people are unhappy at work. Among other indicators, low retention in manufacturing companies, especially at the supervisory level is a pretty good indication of this. In my consulting work, I see this in other places as well. People seem to just go through the motions, they do the minimum, they see work as a means to an end, and they don't like the job they do or the people they work with.

In my humble opinion, if people aren't where they want to be,

---

[60] https://www.wmar2news.com/lifestyle/80-percent-of-americans-dont-like-their-jobs

[61] https://www.theladders.com/career-advice/majority-unhappy-at-work

they are 100 percent responsible for that. They have decided, based on their own assessment of themselves what kind of life they deserve, what goals they can achieve, what job they will do, how much money they make, etc. If a person is not happy with his/her life. He/she needs to make a change.

Apparently, the research disagrees with me and suggests that only about 40 percent of our happiness is under our own control; the rest is determined by genetics and external factors[62]. Even if this is true, there is still a lot we can do to control our own happiness.

Whether it's 40 percent or 100 percent of outcomes that we can control, we will have the ability to make choices. This knowing that we have the ability to direct our own life is called personal power. And when we acknowledge that power, we are taking responsibility. Grownups at work must learn to take responsibility. If supervisors want individuals on their teams to be responsible, the supervisor must be to adopt this social competence strategy and lead by example.

This is one area where many supervisors fall short. And it's not always their fault. Frequently in manufacturing, for example, employees who had no intention of being supervisors find themselves in the role and this is the reason they are unhappy. Being promoted to a job you didn't want is so common there is a name for it, it's called The Peter Principle. (By the way, if you are interested in a career in manufacturing, there is a lot of opportunity. By 2025, the skills gap in the manufacturing industry is expected to grow to two million, **according to Deloitte**, and 82 percent of executives believe that it will affect their ability to meet their customers' needs[63]).

---

[62] https://www.businessinsider.com/happiness-behaviours-characteristics-science-2017-7?r=UK

[63] https://belflex.com/2017/06/08/improving-retention-in-the-manufacturing-industry/

The Peter Principle references an observation that the tendency in most organizational **hierarchies**, such as that of a corporation, is for every employee to rise in the hierarchy through promotion until they reach a level of respective incompetence. In other words, a front-office secretary who is quite good at her job may thus be promoted to executive assistant to the **CEO** for which she is not trained or prepared for—meaning that she would be more productive for the company (and likely herself) if she had not been promoted.

The Peter Principle is thus based on the logical idea that competent **employees** will continue to be promoted, but at some point will be promoted into positions for which they are incompetent, and they will then remain in those positions because of the fact that they do not demonstrate any further competence that would get them recognized for additional promotion. According to the Peter Principle, every position in a given hierarchy will eventually be filled by employees who are incompetent to fulfill the job duties of their respective positions. Most people will not turn down a promotion, especially if it comes with greater pay and prestige—even if they know they are unqualified for the position[64].

Regardless of whether you wanted to be in a role or not, once you accept that role, you must take personal responsibility for that choice and then act accordingly.

Key Take-Away

It does not matter what people say. People say all kinds of things for all kinds of reasons and you can't put a lot of stock into words. However, **how a person acts, usually tells you what he/she really thinks**, what his/her goals and values are, and who he/she is as a person. We each have the power to make choices and devise a life we are proud of, and where we are is a reflection of our choices.

---

[64] https://www.investopedia.com/terms/p/peter-principle.asp

Social Competence Skill that Supervisors Need: Personal Responsibility

Taking responsibility is different than being accountable. Supervisors must do both, but these are two different things.

Taking Responsibility at Work Means:

- ☐ Recognizing that there are aspects of the work e.g., tasks and/or processes based on role and job description, that are your individual assignment.
- ☐ Acknowledging that there are aspects of work, e.g., personal management basics that are your responsibility without being assigned, e.g.,
    - o Be on time
    - o Dress appropriately
    - o Manage your own health and stress
    - o Build rapport
    - o Solve your own personal problems
    - o Act like an adult, e.g., be professional, show restraint

Note: taking responsibility happens *before and while* the work gets done.

On the job, taking responsibility looks like:

- ☐ Saying what you mean (integrity) and doing what you say (follow through)
- ☐ Realizing that others may share similar responsibilities (tasks) but you are each required to complete/fulfill your separate parts
- ☐ Knowing that in workplaces, every individual is responsible for him/herself but also, generally responsible for each other, e.g., keep each other safe

Being accountable means:

- ☐ Recognizing that your contributions (what you are

responsible for) are a necessary and important part of the overall goals of the team and of the organization.
- ☐ Expecting to be measured/evaluated and held to a predetermined standard

On the job, being accountable looks like:

- ☐ Understanding you have obligations: moral, ethical, and legal to your co-workers, higherups and the organization
- ☐ Taking ownership of something
- ☐ Accepting responsibility when things don't go well
- ☐ Anticipating being measured
- ☐ Expecting to be held accountable
- ☐ Following guidelines and rules e.g., safety
- ☐ Living the organizational values e.g., ethics, honesty

Note: Being accountable happens *after* the work gets done. Taking responsibility and being accountable will usually help you keep your job and often get you promoted. And if you are a supervisor, there is something else you can do to get promoted. Good supervisors make their boss's jobs easier. The more you do the little things, the unexpected, the tasks that fall under your list of accountabilities and authority but are not directly assigned, the quicker you can establish yourself as someone who shows initiatives but still respects hierarchy. This makes you promotable.

How Do You Teach Personal Responsibility?

One responsibility when you are a supervisor is to hold your team accountable for the outcomes of their actions. Most responsible adults expect to have their performance measured on the job, and if they are responsible, they look forward to being evaluated because they accept responsibility for their own development and personal growth. They also know they are accountable to the team and to the employer to do so.

As a supervisor, you must show that you too are responsible. In this way, others can learn by watching you. And as a supervisor part of your job is to hold others accountable for fulfilling their responsibilities. In cases where individuals do not exhibit personal responsibility you can also teach them by:

- Giving people as much information as possible
- Providing ongoing opportunities for learning
- Giving clear and direct instructions and expectations and hopefully having time also giving reasons why you are giving those instructions.
- Working to build rapport and trust such that if there is a time constraint and you do not have enough time to explain why you are asking someone to do a task, the employee trusts you at the present time and knows that you will be able to give more information when time allows.
- Showing you are personally responsible, e.g., for your own health
- Measuring performance ongoing, show people when they are meeting expectations
- Coaching others when you identify shortfalls
- Assigning tasks based on skill level and/or capacity, e.g., don't give responsibilities that are beyond skill levels
- Letting people make low-risk decisions
- Letting people self-direct, e.g., how to do a task
- Encouraging solutions-oriented thinking
- Challenging people to try new things
- Avoiding micro-managing
- Acknowledging when people meet expectations
- Empowering others to challenge themselves
- Holding people accountable

Masotti Common Sense Social Competence Strategy #10 – Be Responsible

☐ Run your own race: Decide what you want out of life and make a plan to achieve it.

- ☐ Establish personal standards e.g.,
    - ○ Morning routine
    - ○ Daily exercise
    - ○ Eat healthy
    - ○ Only take jobs that pay a minimum of X
    - ○ Do not engage in, or endorse, illegal activity
    - ○ Pay what I owe
- ☐ Establish personal policies, e.g.,
    - ○ Do not lie
    - ○ Always do more than is expected
    - ○ Always consider how my actions will impact others
    - ○ Never steal
    - ○ Always save someone else some hardship or misery if I can
    - ○ Give without expecting anything in return
- ☐ Clarify expectations of others
- ☐ Make promises, but only if you can keep them
- ☐ Learn to say no
- ☐ Learn to apologize
- ☐ Accept compliments
- ☐ Accept apologies from others
- ☐ Invite feedback
- ☐ Learn from mistakes
- ☐ Forgive yourself for mistakes
- ☐ Accept that you can't fix/help/save everyone; people must learn to take responsibility for themselves
- ☐ Be sure you know what your specific responsibilities are, e.g., job tasks
- ☐ Take ownership of our own learning

Please see Chapter 11 for Sources and Resources for ongoing learning.

Chapter 11
Sources and Resources

Introduction

Production Supervisor Job Responsibilities: Manufactures products by supervising staff; organizing and monitoring workflow.

Production Supervisor Job Duties:
- Accomplishes manufacturing staff results by communicating job expectations; planning, monitoring, and appraising job results; coaching, counseling, and disciplining employees; initiating, coordinating, and enforcing systems, policies, and procedures.

- Maintains staff by recruiting, selecting, orienting, and training employees; developing personal growth opportunities.

- Maintains work flow by monitoring steps of the process; setting processing variables; observing control points and equipment; monitoring personnel and resources; studying methods; implementing cost reductions; developing reporting procedures and systems; facilitating corrections to malfunctions within process control points; initiating and fostering a spirit of cooperation within and between departments.

- Completes production plan by scheduling and assigning personnel; accomplishing work results; establishing priorities; monitoring progress; revising schedules; resolving problems; reporting results of the processing flow on shift production summaries.

- Maintains quality service by establishing and enforcing organization standards.

- Ensures operation of equipment by calling for repairs; evaluating new equipment and techniques.

- Provides manufacturing information by compiling, initiating, sorting, and analyzing production performance records and data; answering questions and responding to requests.

- Creates and revises systems and procedures by analyzing operating practices, record-keeping systems, forms of control, and budgetary and personnel requirements; implementing change.

- Maintains safe and clean work environment by educating and directing personnel on the use of all control points, equipment, and resources; maintaining compliance with established policies and procedures.

- Maintains working relationship with the union by following the terms of the collective bargaining agreement.

- Resolves personnel problems by analyzing data; investigating issues; identifying solutions; recommending action.

- Maintains professional and technical knowledge by attending educational workshops; reviewing professional publications; establishing personal networks; benchmarking state-of-the-art practices; participating in professional societies.

- Contributes to team effort by accomplishing related results as needed.

Production Supervisor Skills and Qualifications:
Supervision, Coaching, Managing Processes, Process Improvement, Tracking Budget Expenses, Production Planning, Controls and Instrumentation, Strategic Planning, Dealing with Complexity, Financial Planning and Strategy, Automotive Manufacturing.

Chapter 1

- *The Power of Pausing*, blog: https://www.briantracy.com/blog/sales-success/the-power-of-pausing/
- Are you a judgmental person- free online assessment **https://www.quizony.com/are-you-a-judgmental-person/index.html**
- Samples of unconscious bias – learn more at: **https://lattice.com/library/how-to-reduce-unconscious-bias-at-work**
    - ☐ The halo effect
    - ☐ The similarity bias
    - ☐ Gender bias
    - ☐ Confirmation bias
    - ☐ "Bropropriating"
    - ☐ Height discrimination
    - ☐ Preferring or favoring certain names or types of names, e.g., culturally based or familiar

- Ten Tips for Being Nonjudgmental, **https://tybennett.com/10-tips-for-being-nonjudgmental/**

These 10 tips for being nonjudgmental from Sheri Van Dijk can help make the distinction.

1. Remember that being nonjudgmental isn't about turning a positive into a negative; it's about being neutral, neither positive nor negative.

2. Reducing your negative judgments will reduce your level of anger and other painful emotions.

3. Keep in mind that judging is like adding fuel to the fire of your emotion; it only increases your painful emotions.

4. You can often reduce a behaviour just by counting how often you're engaging in that behaviour. If you get overwhelmed or discouraged by the thought of stopping your judging, start by counting your judgments first then work your way toward changing them.

5. Remember that being nonjudgmental will not only help you reduce your emotional pain but will also have a positive impact on your relationships.

6. We often respond to a situation as though our judgments were true rather than just labels we've stuck on something or someone.

7. Remember the learning curve: at first, you'll notice your judgments only after you've made them. As you continue practicing, however you'll notice them as you're making them – before you say them out loud and as they form in your head – until gradually, you'll find you're able to form nonjudgmental statements naturally before a judgment arises within you.

8. As with any skill, being nonjudgmental will be more difficult when your emotions are high.

9. Practice observing-your-thoughts exercises to help you become more aware of your judgments.

10. Don't judge yourself for judging. It's human nature!

- The Secret to Self-Restraint (YouTube)
  https://www.youtube.com/watch?v=tTb3d5cjSFI

Chapter 2

- **The Civility Toolkit** (1000 tools related to civility)
  www.civilitycenter.org/toolkit

- **Recommended Reading:** *The 30% Solution, How Civility at Work Can Increase Engagement, Retention and Profitability*, Lewena Bayer
- **13 Ways to Make Employees Feel Valued** (full article at **https://hrdailyadvisor.blr.com/2018/12/27/how-to-make-employees-feel-valued/**
    - Give Recognition
    - Provide Feedback
    - Solicit Opinion
    - Communicate Frequently
    - Give Direct Compensation
    - Give Benefits the Employees Chooses
    - Provide Opportunity for Peer Praise
    - Show Appreciation
    - Public Recognition
    - Say Thank You
    - Provide Challenging Work
    - Celebrate Success and Anniversaries
    - Invest in Continued Development
- **Imposter Syndrome Test** (You don't have to fake it- you know more than you think)
https://testyourself.psychtests.com/testid/3803
- **Definition of civility** by Civility Experts Inc.

CIVILITY IS:
A conscious awareness of the impact of one's thoughts, actions, words and intentions on others; combined with, A continuous acknowledgement of one's responsibility to ease the experience of others (e.g., through restraint, kindness, non-judgment, respect, and courtesy); and, A consistent effort to adopt and exhibit civil behaviour as a non-negotiable point of one's character. – Lewena Bayer, CEO Civility Experts Inc.

Chapter 3

- Howard Gardner's **Multiple Intelligence Theory**
  Snapshot;
  http://karlalbrecht.com/articles/pages/socialintelligence.htm

	Category	Description
A	Abstract Intelligence	Symbolic Reasoning
S	Social Intelligence	Dealing with people
P	Practical Intelligence	Getting things done
E	Emotional Intelligence	Self-awareness and self-management
A	Aesthetic Intelligence	Sense of form, design, music, art and literature
K	Kinesthetic Intelligence	Whole-body skills like sports, dance or flying a jet fighter

- **Recommended Reading**, Social IQ, The New Science of Success, K. Albrecht.
- Partial list of triggering symptoms for **Social Phobia Disorder https://socialphobia.org/social-anxiety-disorder-definition-symptoms-treatment-therapy-medications-insight-prognosis**

- Being introduced to other people
- Being teased or criticized
- Being the center of attention
- Being watched or observed while doing something
- Having to say something in a formal, public situation
- Meeting people in authority ("important people/authority figures")
- Feeling insecure and out of place in social situations ("I don't know what to say.")
- Embarrassing easily (e.g., blushing, shaking)
- Meeting other peoples' eyes
- Swallowing, writing, talking, making phone calls if in public

Chapter 4

- Great article on **Tribal Knowledge in Manufacturing** https://www.industryweek.com/talent/recruiting-retention/article/22007278/a-strategy-to-capture-tribal-knowledge
- Some interesting **facts about listening**:
  - **85 percent** of what we have learned is through listening (not talking or reading).(Shorpe)
  - **75 percent** of the time, we are distracted, preoccupied or forgetful. (Hunsaker)
  - After listening to someone talk, we can *immediately* recall about **50 percent** of what was said. Even less is we didn't like the subject or the person! (Robinson)

- One hour later, we remember less than **20 percent** of what we heard. (Shorpe)
- Less than **2 percent** of the population has had formal educational on how to listen. (Gregg)
- We **listen** at 125-250 words per minute, but **think** at 1000-3000 words per minute. (HighGain, Inc.)

  https://transforminc.com/2014/07/interesting-facts-listening/

- **7 Qualities of a Good Mentor**
  https://www.themuse.com/advice/how-to-find-qualities-good-mentor
- **Continuous Learning Self-Assessment - HRSDC.CA/EssentialSkills**

Continuous learning is about expanding your ability to learn by regularly upgrading your skills and increasing your knowledge. Strong **continuous learning** skills are required to successfully adapt to changing work and life demands. Complete this self-assessment to help you understand your **continuous learning** strengths and areas for improvement.

Instructions:

1. Read each statement in **Section 1** and place a check mark in the column that **best** describes how well you can complete that task. **Tip:** THINK ABOUT YOUR WORK AND LIFE EXPERIENCES AS YOU CONSIDER EACH TASK.

2. Review your response for each task. If you have checked seven or more in the "Somewhat" and/or "No"

columns, you may want to consider upgrading your **continuous learning** skills.

3. Complete **Section 2** to identify your **continuous learning** strengths and areas for improvement.

Section 1: Self-Assessment

Section 1: Self-Assessment			
I can...	Yes	Some-what	No
Learn new things.			
Ask questions when I do not understand something.			
Ask for feedback and/or advice from more experienced co-workers.			
Identify learning or training programs that are available to me at work and in my community.			
Learn by observing more experienced co-workers.			
Find and use learning materials and/or resources (e.g. searching the Internet, reading articles).			
Seek out and participate in training courses.			
Identify and understand my skill strengths and the areas			

where I need improvement.			
Develop my own learning goals at work and in my personal life.			
Apply the lessons I have learned from past experiences to new situations.			
Try new ways of doing things.			
Use newly learned skills and knowledge to improve my work.			
Recognize my preferred learning style (e.g. learning by seeing, hearing or doing).			
Be responsible for my own learning.			
Maintain my skill levels by practicing what I have learned.			
TOTAL			

Chapter 5

- The **Honest-Humility Factor** has been used in a variety of studies as a measure of ethical or pro-social behaviour Ashton and Lee (2008). Low levels of the Honesty-Humility factor are associated with greater levels of materialism, unethical business practices and deviant sexual behaviour. The Honesty-Humility factor has been found to predict endorsement of unethical business practices and even the degree to which a person will take health and safety risks (even towards fellow employees). An individual

who scores low on the Honesty-Humility factor may have a proclivity for anti-social acts. Which anti-social acts an individual is likely to commit may be related to their personality profile along the other factors of the HEXACO model. For example, someone who scores low on Honesty-Humility and low on Conscientiousness and Agreeableness are more likely to engage in delinquency in the workplace.
Ashton, M. C.; Lee, K. (2008). "The HEXACO Model of Personality Structure and the Importance of the H Factor". *Social and Personality Psychology Compass*. **2** (5): 1952.

☐ **Recommended Reading**: *The Speed of Trust*, S. Covey
https://www.speedoftrust.com/

☐ **How trustworthy are you?** Free assessment: For those who want to assess their trustworthiness, visit **http://trustedadvisor.com/trustQuotient/dm**. The self-assessment includes 20 questions, takes about five minutes, and is free. The TQ assessment provides tips on how you can improve your trustworthiness in each of four characteristics.

☐ **Nonverbal Communication- 5 Purposes**

- **Repetition:** It repeats and often strengthens the message you're making verbally.

- **Contradiction:** It can contradict the message you're trying to convey, thus indicating to your listener that you may not be telling the truth.

- **Substitution:** It can substitute for a verbal message. For example, your facial expression often conveys a far more vivid message than words ever can.

- **Complementing:** It may add to or complement your verbal message. As a boss, if you pat an employee on the back in addition to giving praise, it can increase the impact of your message.

- **Accenting:** It may accent or underline a verbal message. Pounding the table, for example, can underline the importance of your message

- Source: THE IMPORTANCE OF EFFECTIVE COMMUNICATION, Edward G. Wertheim, Ph.D.

Chapter 6

- Robin Sharma, article on **Listening** https://www.robinsharma.com/article/listen-carefully
- Forbes – **21 Principles of Persuasion** https://www.forbes.com/sites/jasonnazar/2013/03/26/the-21-principles-of-persuasion/#4106e286a4c9
- **Attention Span Facts** e.g., According to scientists, the age of smartphones has left humans with such a short attention span even a goldfish can hold a thought for longer. Researchers surveyed 2,000 participants in Canada and studied the brain activity of 112 others using electroencephalograms.
The results showed the average human attention span has fallen from 12 seconds in 2000, or around the time the mobile revolution began, to eight seconds. Goldfish, meanwhile,

are believed to have an attention span of nine seconds.
https://www.telegraph.co.uk/science/2016/03/12/humans-have-shorter-attention-span-than-goldfish-thanks-to-smart/

- **Barriers to Listening** http://www.free-management-ebooks.com/faqcm/active-05.htm

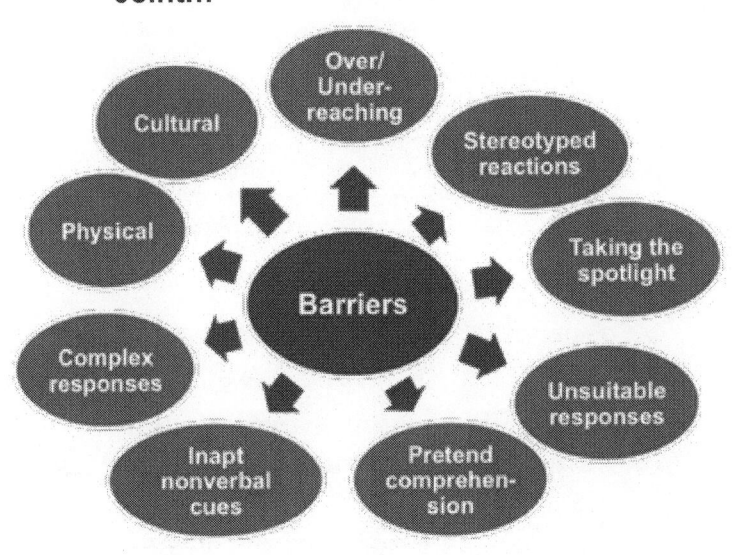

Barriers diagram: Cultural, Over/Under-reaching, Stereotyped reactions, Taking the spotlight, Unsuitable responses, Pretend comprehension, Inapt nonverbal cues, Complex responses, Physical

Chapter 7

- **Angela Duckworth on "GRIT"**
  https://www.newharbinger.com/blog/what-grit-and-why-it-important

  Grit is passion and perseverance for long-term and meaningful goals.

  It is the ability to persist in something you feel passionate about and persevere when you face obstacles. This kind of passion is not about intense emotions or infatuation. It's about having direction and commitment. When you have this kind of passion, you can stay committed to a task that may be difficult or boring. Grit is also about perseverance. To persevere means to stick with it; to continue working hard even after experiencing difficulty or failure.

- Article on Impact of **Mental Fatigue** https://www.physiology.org/doi/full/10.1152/japplphysiol.91324.2008
- **Resilience Assessment** Developed by Andrew C. Weis, Ph.D., LP. Last revised 3.15.2010 Resilience is the ability to bounce back from difficulty, to navigate difficult challenges with awareness, intention, and skill. Resilience develops naturally through connections to others, balanced self-care, and an open and engaged mind.

Rate yourself on the items below, using the following scale:
<u>In the past year</u>, how often has this statement been true for you?
1 = Never or rarely
2 = Sometimes
3 = Often
4 = Always or almost always

Connections	I am close to at least one person, whom I trust and will seek for support.	1 2 3 4
Benefiting Others	I contribute to the wellbeing of others.	1 2 3 4
Physical Self-	I exercise aerobically three or more days a	1 2 3 4

Care	week, sleep enough to have energy throughout the day, spend at least an hour a day outdoors, and eat a balanced, moderate, and wholesome diet including five or more servings of fruits and vegetables a day.	
Stress Reduction Practice	Four or more days a week, I participate in at least one practice to quiet my mind and body. *(Examples: deep breathing, time in nature, playing a musical instrument, yoga, meditation, prayer, journaling, tai chi, qigong, progressive muscle relaxation, autogenic training*	1 2 3 4
Flexible Thinking	When I am going through a difficult time, I consider multiple perspectives on it as well as multiple options for responding to it.	1 2 3 4
Self-confidence	I trust myself, my intuition, and my abilities.	1 2 3 4
Openness to Experience	I seek and enjoy new and unfamiliar experiences.	1 2 3 4
Workability	I approach every challenge as though I	1 2 3 4

	can work through it somehow.	
Awareness	I notice the world around me, and I can often anticipate opportunities and challenges because of what I notice.	1 2 3 4
Experience Facing Big Challenges	I have faced difficult challenges before and have found healthy and adaptive ways to work through them.	1 2 3 4
Willingness	When challenges arise, I face them and I <u>do not</u> deny them, ignore them, or use alcohol or other drugs to avoid or cope with them.	1 2 3 4
Engagement	I engage in one or more activities that focus my attention and efforts <u>and</u> that deeply satisfy me.	1 2 3 4
Big Picture	I keep perspective on my challenges by considering the bigger picture.	1 2 3 4
		Score:

Assessing Your View of Your Resilience

Score	Assessment
36 or higher	You are likely to view yourself as resilient, and if your view is accurate, you are likely to thrive in the face of challenges and could serve as a strong support and role-model for others.
27 – 35	You are likely to view yourself as having typical resilience, and you will likely do fine with most challenges. Unless you are selling yourself short on your assessment, you have some room for enhancing your resilience.
26 or lower	You are likely to view yourself as not very resilient. You have ample room for enhancing your resilience. Lower scores are common among people who have had few challenges early in life or have been overwhelmed by challenges early in life. History is not destiny.

Enhancing Your Resilience

1. Identify the items in the Resilience Self-Assessment which you could most readily enhance. The items are written not only to assess but to relay enough information to help you enhance that aspect of resilience.
2. Balance between building existing strengths and addressing your greatest vulnerabilities (i.e., lowest scores). Note that items are not in any particular order, but in general healthy connections to others have proven most predictive of resilience.
3. Learn more about resilience. An excellent first resource is *The Road to Resilience* **a brochure published by the American Psychological Association and available free** http://www.apa.org/HELPCENTER/road-resilience.aspx

4. <u>Ask for support</u> in your efforts to enhance your resilience.
5. <u>Trust your approach</u> to enhancing your resilience. Some people do best with making a plan first. Some people do best by jumping right in. Some people do best with one change at a time. Some people do best making multiple changes at once.
6. <u>Make adjustments</u> if your approach isn't working for you. Try a different focus. Ask for different support or ask for support from others you might not have first considered for support.

Chapter 8

- **Collaboration Pyramid**
  http://www.nfusion.com/article/thought-leadership-building-a-culture-of-collaboration

- **Reasons why collaboration fails:**
  https://www.smartsheet.com/collaborative-teamwork

Collaboration for Superior Results

The demand for a collaborative work product is only increasing, and the amount of time the workforce spends in team-related activities will also continue to increase, according to author Jeanne Meister. Even though it has become crucial to workplace success, however, collaboration is often difficult.

Workplace failures can happen when collaboration and team skills are absent. Your business can end up as an incohesive collection of competing silos, departments, and individuals. Without strong collaboration and communication skills, you can lose productivity and money. You need to add in other skill sets, such as decision-making and leadership to guide your group. Some other factors that can tank your team include:

- **Forcing Collaboration:** People can resent forced collaboration when they aren't given clear evidence as to why the players make sense. Collaborations that come together naturally are often best because everyone understands what everyone else is bringing to the table.
- **A Bad Team History:** If these people had a negative experience working together in the past, it's best to determine the reason as quickly as possible. Ask the hard questions early on to find out if leadership (or something else) was the issue. Repeating history will not yield a positive outcome.
- **Poor Relationships:** Even the best-structured groups can suffer if you have two or more team members who do not get along. You can mitigate this problem by limiting their interaction and designing group standards for meetings and

communication. Some people will never get along - this is fine if everyone can comport themselves like professionals. If they cannot behave appropriately, perhaps they have no place on your team.

- **Ineffective Meetings:** Meetings without structure can cause your staff to have conversations that spin without purpose. Structure your meetings so that your staff knows the purpose and agenda going in. In addition, you should agree upon the meeting deliverables from the outset (i.e., either before or at the beginning of the meeting).
- **Little Transparency or Inadequate Information Sharing:** When you have team members whose work depends on that of other team members, they need to share their progress, concerns, and barriers. In order to stimulate this sharing, you need to develop trust among your members. Transparency goes a long way toward accomplishing trust.
- **No Team Governance Processes:** Maintaining structure keeps everyone on the same page. They know what to expect, have standards of communication and behaviour, and are able to settle disputes. Setting up structured processes early and with the buy-in of your team helps keep disagreements to a minimum.

- **Conflicting Styles of Decision Making:** People process information differently. Some people process information quickly and are able to respond with an answer right away. Some people need to process away from the group and think slowly through all the options. Styles of decision making can differ significantly and cause eruptions of frustration.
- **Behind-the-Scenes Conversations and Processes:** Conversations and processes that cut others out erode the trust and confidence of your team. When you communicate outside the agreed-upon group settings or make decisions outside the group processes, it puts your project at risk.
- **Competition:** Competition is the opposite of collaboration. The spirit of competition requires people to withhold information, work ahead of others when they are capable, and actively try to exploit the weakness in their competitors. Competition within a team meant to be collaborative is inappropriate unless structured very carefully.
- **Turf Wars:** Akin to competition, turf wars often bring about the opposite of the desired effect. One of the main benefits of collaboration is that people (even with vastly different skill sets) can mentor and teach each other their skills. Breaking down barriers, whether they are

between departments or individuals, builds everyone's knowledge base.
- **Poor Ownership or Engagement among Team Members:** One main tenant of developing a collaborative group is that you develop buy-in from the team. This includes buy-in concerning the process, direction, and expected outcomes. If your team is not engaged, they will not be able to identify problems as they arise and will miss valuable opportunities.

Chapter 9

- ☐ YouTube video on **40 percent Rule** https://thehustle.co/40-percent-rule-navy-seal-secret-mental-toughness
- ☐ **Self Awareness Supports** http://www.pathwaytohappiness.com/self-awareness.htm Self Awareness is having a clear perception of your personality, including strengths, weaknesses, thoughts, beliefs, motivation, and emotions. Self-Awareness allows you to understand other people, how they perceive you, your attitude and your responses to them in the moment.

  We might quickly assume that we are self-aware, but it is helpful to have a relative scale for awareness. If you have ever been in an auto accident you may have experienced everything happening in slow motion and noticing details of your thought process and the event. This is a state if heightened awareness. With practice we can learn to engage these types of heightened states and see new opportunities for interpretations in our thoughts, emotions, and conversations.

- ☐ **Communicating Confidence Tip Sheet Civility**

Experts Inc

How we talk, our tone of voice, speech style and the vocabulary we use says a lot about who we are. Whoever is listening can often pick up clues about how much we really know, how strongly we feel about something and how much self- confidence we have just by listening to the words we use and how we use them. It's important to learn how our body language along with can the words we use can help us to communicate to others that we are positive and happy. The only challenge can be those words and phrases that show the opposite. Here are some examples:

The following words say, "I'm not entirely sure" or "I'm not too confident" or "I'm not feeling very optimistic": maybe, sorry, no!, that's not possible, huh?, sometimes, but..., hmm..., I can't..., #$@(*&^, never, always, what?

These words say "I'm confident", "I'm positive", "I'm confident".... yes!, thank you, I'll find out, let's see, I can, If...then...., what about..., please, I will, I want to.

When we speak to others, especially someone who is angry or upset, we want to use language that shows concern and a willingness to help, however, we do not want to take personal responsibility for things beyond our control and we do not want to appear incompetent or wimpy in our communications with them.

Chapter 10

- **Daniel Pink, The Surprising Truth About What Motivates Us.**
  https://www.youtube.com/watch?v=u6XAPnuFjJc
- **ACCOUNTABILITY WEBSITES:**
  http://www.amanet.org/training/articles/No-Excuses-Being-Accountable-for-Your-Own-Success.aspx
  http://www.audreymarlene-lifecoach.com/taking-responsibility.html
  http://www.toddherman.com/personal-accountability
- **Recommended Reading:** *How Did That Happen?*

AUTHOR: Roger Connors and Tom Smith
LINK: http://www.amazon.com/How-Did-That-Happen-Accountable-ebook/dp/B002IPZJ9M/ref=sr_1_2?s=books&ie=UTF8&qid=1398561558&sr=1-2&keywords=accountable
BLURB: Surprises caused by a lack of personal accountability plague almost every organization today, from the political arena to large and small businesses. How Did That Happen? offers a proven way to eliminate these nasty surprises, gain an unbeatable competitive edge, and enhance performance by holding others accountable the positive, principled way.

☐ **ACCOUNTABILITY COURSES:**
https://www.soundviewpro.com/online-courses/_/installing-an-accountability-based-culture-for-success?gclid=CMaF-qG5_70CFbFaMgodICkAPA
http://theaccountabilityproject.ca/courses/
http://www.ozprinciple.com/webinar/

Three Phones and A Radio – Terms and Definitions

1. **Situational Blindness**
   The inability to see what is right in front of you, e.g., in a workplace setting. Situational blindness typically results from low social radar skills and can result in spending unnecessary time doing, or thinking about, things that need not be done at all. In manufacturing and example is when a supervisor fails to consider that the members of his team likely have the answers to a problem he is trying to solve and so rather than ask his team, he spends a lot of time looking for answers that are right in front of him.

2. **Social Acuity**
   A term used by Civility Experts Inc. that describes the level of accuracy and consistency with which a person can apply his/her social intelligence., e.g., how sharp is a person's perception of the overall tone of a room or the unspoken messages, or the "feel" of a scenario.[65]

3. **Off Standard Behaviour**
   References a situation, behaviour, gesture, approach, etc. that is not typical, that is, different from what you have come to understand as normal or standard.

4. **Restraint**
   A physical halt use in the Massoti Commonsense Social Competence Strategy "wait for it". The halt may include a verbal pause, being quiet, holding still, and/or to take no action for a measured amount of time.

5. **Brain-restraint**
   Psychological restraint, which means suspending judgment and avoiding jumping to conclusions. Of course, your general brain activity doesn't stop, the idea is that you deliberately stall aspects of your thinking patterns or habits. For just a few minutes, don't think. Experience and observe calmly and keep a neutral mindset. You deliberately stall aspects of your thinking patterns or habits.

6. **People Treatment**
   People treatment is a civility term that refers to an overall attitude about what constitutes a fair and good way of interaction with people. It includes how you speak, nonverbal gestures, the extent to which you are

---

[65] Lewena Bayer

empathetic, and how you define honesty and integrity. An individual's idea of people treatment can vary from one context to another.[66]

7. **Shared Information Bias**
Refers to how individuals in a nice workplace learn that one of the best ways of making a group feel good and making their teammates see then as competent is to repeat and repackage information that everyone already knows. It makes the person sharing look smart and in-step with his/her colleagues even if he/she is just rehashing the same thing that was said last week or by a person who spoke a moment prior.[67]

8. **Relational Wealth**
A civility term used by Civility Experts Inc. that refers to the invaluable benefits of strong connections e.g., via interpersonal relationships. The terms relates to Lew Bayer, CEO Civility Experts Inc. suggestion that *"Collaboration is currency in the new world of work"*.[68]

9. **Civility**
A conscious awareness of the impact of one's thoughts, actions, words and intentions on others; combined with, a continuous acknowledgement of one's responsibility to ease the experience of others (e.g., through restraint, kindness, non-judgment, respect, and courtesy); and, a consistent effort to adopt and exhibit civil behaviour as a non-negotiable point of one's character.[69]

---

[66] Lewena Bayer

[67] Quartz

[68] Lewena Bayer

[69] Lewena Bayer

10. Social Intelligence

One of four skills that underpin the ability to be civil, according to Civility Experts Inc. Social Intelligence is a cluster of three subskills (social style, social radar, and social knowledge) and one of several intelligences, e.g., kinesthetic, emotional, mathematical etc. Social intelligence is your ability to effectively read and interpret nonverbal, verbal, tonal, and contextual cues in a range of social settings. Social intelligence is critical to building trust and to forming long-lasting relationships. [70]

11. Persona

The qualities and characteristics that you create or build in an effort to fit into a particular situation or role. E.g., if you are not a "rough" person by nature, you might adopt language, gestures or specific postures as a way of projecting sameness with the people around you.

12. Social Competence

Related to civility at work specifically, social competence is a cluster of skills including those below. To be competent socially, an individual is able to apply all of the skills below concurrently and consistently which results in ability to communicate and interact in a way that builds positive, trusting relationships. Social Intelligence
- Personal Management Basics
- Resilience
- Hardiness
- Cultural Competence[71]

---

[70] Lewena Bayer

[71] Lewena Bayer

13. Reverse Social Engineering

This is a social radar strategy where you observe behaviour and make mental or other notes about what you see. Then, when situations or communications don't go as planned, you work backwards. Start with the outcome and recall the gestures, words, tone, and cues that should have hinted or warned you that the exchange was off track. This enables you to recognize those cues in future so that you can adjust your approach as necessary and avoid the undesired outcome.

14. Social Honesty

When a person says what is perceived to be the right thing in a certain context, e.g., when it isn't polite to tell the truth, or when telling the truth is not politically correct or could harm social impression or status. [72]

15. Righteous Honesty

When someone is taking an indignant or defensive stance and so blurts out hurtful honesty, e.g., tells truth about someone else's actions as a means of deflecting from their own dishonesty. [73]

16. Authentic Honesty

When a person tells the truth because being honest is his/her core value, and doing so is the right and good thing to do. In this case, though, partly because the truth-telling is values based, the truth teller considers the *way* the truth comes out, e.g., considering what is

---

[72] Lewena Bayer

[73] Lewena Bayer

appropriate timing, giving the listener some warning etc.[74]

17. End in Mind Listening

A civility term referring going into communications knowing in advance of the conversation what you need to happen after the communication. You may relinquish control of how you get to the desired end point, e.g., you don't assume you know how people will respond, but because the interaction is goal-directed communication, you can ask strategic questions. By using this approach, you will usually get the answers you need quickly and precisely. At the same time you build trust because your motives are transparent and you are direct and fact-based. [75]

18. Resilience

Refers to mental stamina and the ability to bounce back, to regain composure and control, and to move forward in a solutions-focused way. Requires personal strength, grit, fidelity of character and a positive outlook. – CM

19. Hardiness

Refers to your physical stamina, your ability to endure harsh conditions and maintain a standard of performance. – CM

---

[74] Lewena Bayer

[75] Lewena

INDICATORS OF SOCIAL ACUITY

Leaders need to have high "social acuity" – that is they need to have a keen social sense. They must be consistently accurate and timely in their perceptions and assessments of social settings. They need to know how to:

- Read contextual cues
- Be attentive to the nuances of workplace culture
- Navigate politics in union environments
- Identify who will be an ally and who will be a challenge
- Build trust
- Repair when a trust is broken
- Consider contextual aspects when timing everything from greetings, to feedback to workplace coaching and performance reviews
- Communicate in a way that leaves everyone involved in the interaction feeling valued
- Acknowledge differences that make a difference, e.g., related to gender, culture, generation
- Give timely and effective feedback
- Monitor and manage nonverbal cues to boost credibility and perceived competence
- Adapt supervisory approach and style to meet the needs of individual workers
- Apply adult learning principles
- Maintain credibility as a leader but still be perceived as approachable by the production team

Masotti Commonsense Social Competence Strategy #1: Wait for It.

- ☐ Pause deliberately to assess the situation
- ☐ Resist saying anything immediately
- ☐ Suspend your thoughts, e.g., don't make assumptions, don't jump to conclusions, set aside any bias or expectations
- ☐ Listen to the other person
- ☐ Pay attention to the context, e.g., what is going on around you?
- ☐ Watch the other person's nonverbal cues
- ☐ Ask questions using a calm, polite tone
- ☐ Avoid starting your sentences with "I" in an effort to be other-focused
- ☐ Be self-aware. Pay attention to when you make snap judgments and work to understand why you have jumped to conclusions and then set those judgments aside.

Masotti Commonsense Social Competence Strategy #2: Just Be Nice

- ☐ Pause, wait…take a breath, compose yourself, think about what you will say or do BEFORE you do it.
- ☐ Assume the best of others; try to set aside any personal issues, history with the individual, personal needs, known biases etc.
- ☐ Consider social protocol. What do the social rules (written or unwritten) suggest is the appropriate response or behaviour in this setting and/or situation?
- ☐ Think about what you want to happen next, e.g., how do you want to be perceived, how do you want the other person to feel, what do you want the outcome of the interaction/communication to be?

- ☐ Consider the time and place, e.g., is this the right time for the communication? Should you go somewhere private? Do you need a 3rd party to witness? Does the other party need time to compose him/herself?
- ☐ Be kind;
    - ☐ Choose words and/or actions that show you at your best and do not cause harm to the other person
    - ☐ Make eye contact as a way of acknowledging others
    - ☐ Extend general greetings, e.g., say hello
    - ☐ Maintain a calm and moderate tone, e.g., don't yell
    - ☐ Avoid swearing
- ☐ Close with a verbal or physical handshake, e.g., shake hands, say thank you for X, look the person in the eye. OR, acknowledge and close the interaction verbally, e.g., say, "So, we are all good then?", or "See you tomorrow then" or something to show you anticipate a positive and future interaction.

Masotti Commonsense Social Competence Strategy #3: Get Out There and Talk to People

- ☐ Always keep your head up when passing others or walking through a workspace, halls, parking lot etc.
- ☐ Even if you don't know people, make it your habit to glance at them. Practice noticing things about people; what they're wearing, expressions etc.
- ☐ Practice keeping an approachable, friendly look on your face.
- ☐ Be deliberate about exhibiting open postures: don't sit with your arms crossed, take your hands out of your pockets, remove sunglasses when talking to people indoors, extend an open palm for a handshake.
- ☐ When you know people (even if you don't know their names) make eye contact and smile.

- ☐ If you can't stop to talk, wave or nod hello, but don't ask a question such as, "How are you?" while you continue walking or moving.
- ☐ If you have time to stop and chat. Stop. Turn your shoulders square with the other person, greet him/her, move to within 24 inches of the other person, and engage. Set aside all other distractions while you do so.
- ☐ If you have to break eye contact or move your attention to someone or something else for a minute, e.g., check your watch, or acknowledge another person, say, "excuse me" before you do it, or say, "sorry about that" after you do it.
- ☐ As you are chatting, make a point to focus on the other person. Ask him/her questions and wait for the answers. Try to avoid talking about yourself.
- ☐ If you didn't shake hands when you greeted the person, and when context and culture suggests its appropriate, extend an exit handshake.
- ☐ If you are legitimately busy, don't stop and pretend to pay attention. Simply state that you are glad to see the person, but are unable to visit at this time, and then wish the person a happy day and move on.

Masotti Commonsense Social Competence Strategy #4
Apply Continuous Learning to Connect with People

- ☐ Treat people with respect from the beginning so that when you need to approach them for help, they see you as someone they can trust who values them.
- ☐ Assume that someone, at some time, somewhere has experienced this same situation.
- ☐ Assume that you are not the only person to have an idea.
- ☐ Always ask the people doing the job, ask them directly, face-to-face.
- ☐ Approach people at the appropriate time.

- Be respectful in your tone, don't assume people have an obligation to help you just because you are a supervisor.
- Ask targeted questions e.g., not open ended.
- Admit you need help.
- Listen for answer- don't interrupt, don't criticize or apply your personal biases, opinions or beliefs.
- Don't dismiss anyone, you never know what information will be useful down the road, even if the information being shared at the time is not relevant, use the interaction as an opportunity to build rapport and trust.
- Consider that one person may not have all the answers, but the collective probably does.
- Acknowledge the sharing and the information, let the person sharing with you know you appreciate their help.
- Give credit when you use the information down the road.
- Share the information with others, e.g., don't hoard it now that you have it.
- Avoid going back to the same person more than once, this can cause strain within the team. Instead build a relationship with each member of the team, this builds credibility.

Masotti Commonsense Social Competence Strategy #5 – Always Tell the Truth

If you want to build trust, here are some communication habits you should adopt:

- Make a point to be honest with everyone- not just some people
- Be consistent, e.g., always tell the truth- don't pick and choose when to be honest
- Be honest when delivering both good and bad news

- Be direct, tell the whole truth versus a piece or version of the truth, e.g., instead of saying you are being fired for lateness, an indirect version, is saying, "You know, lateness is one of the metrics we watch."
- Assume the best of people, but don't immediately trust everything people say, ask strategic questions
- Look people in the eye when you are communicating the truth
- Be deliberate in your communication- choose your words carefully and say exactly what you mean, don't sugarcoat or be vague
- Avoid pretending you have authority or power you don't have- be honest about your abilities and influence
- Do your due diligence before making promises- ensure you can follow through before you say what you can and will do
- Pick an appropriate time to be truthful
- Consider privacy and confidentiality
- Monitor your tone, e.g., don't be harsh
- Avoid apologizing for telling the truth, e.g., "I'm sorry to have to tell you X, but…"
- Give people a minute to absorb what you are telling them
- Keep being truthful, even when others are dishonest, and/or even when no one seems to notice. People do notice, and there is often documentation to support your efforts

Masotti Commonsense Social Competence Strategy #6 – Ask Strategic Questions

- See people as resources. Assume you can learn from them.
- Be clear in your own mind about what exactly you need to know – what information are you seeking?

- Watch for the appropriate time to approach someone to ask questions e.g., don't bother employees right before lunch or during lunch or breaks. This is their personal time and they may resent your intrusion. Consider approaching at the end of the shift or just after a break or lunch.
- Consider privacy and confidentiality.
- Do not interrupt when the other person is talking.
- Don't assume you already know the answer to the question you are asking.
- Don't assume that the answer is correct or factual, be sure.
- Don't assume that only one person has the answer or information you seek. Ask more than one person if possible.
- Don't assume that one person speaks for the whole group.
- Monitor your postures and nonverbal communication when listening e.g., avoid condescending or impatient gestures
- Listen with TING
- Ask a specific question, start with one question only. Avoid bombarding the person with many questions at once.
- Chose a specific question for a specific purpose, e.g.,
    - Ask a how is your day question to gage morale or attitude.
    - Ask a get to the point question to hold someone accountable for a misbehaviour
    - Ask a what would happen if question to get someone to share information or help resolve a problem
- Don't expect a thank you and don't say things like, "You owe me one", extend the gesture with no expectation of reciprocity

Masotti Social Competence Strategy #7 – Build Resilience (Learn to Take a Punch)

- ☐ Show people how the work they do is valued on the job, e.g., why is enduring the hardship worth it?
- ☐ Make people aware of the type of challenges they may face on the job.
- ☐ Provide opportunities for people to see how others managed those challenges in the past.
- ☐ Build your own resilience, e.g., model resilient behaviour for example:
    - o Have a positive attitude
    - o Name your fears, and face them
    - o Set small achievable personal goals ongoing so that you can experience success
    - o Encourage others, e.g., foster optimism
    - o Don't take yourself too seriously, e.g., have a sense of humor
    - o Take advantage of social supports around you, e.g., ask for help when you need it
- ☐ Encourage autonomy
- ☐ Provide opportunities to practice coping strategies
- ☐ Build "time out" opportunities into daily routine, e.g., make sure people get breaks
- ☐ Incorporate positive language, e.g., affirmations, into workplace slogans and mottos
- ☐ Provide team supports, e.g., buddy and mentor programs

Masotti Commonsense Social Competence Strategy #8 – Foster Collaboration

- ☐ Be approachable
- ☐ Don't take yourself too seriously

- ☐ Be able to say "I don't know"
- ☐ Be transparent
- ☐ Assume there are people in the room smarter than you are
- ☐ Acknowledge the experience, skills, and credentials of others
- ☐ Be curious, ask questions
- ☐ Ask for help
- ☐ Take notes, show that you are serious about the information you are seeking
- ☐ Review the process that support collaboration
- ☐ Offer support, with no strings attached
- ☐ Be honest about what you know
- ☐ Share what you know
- ☐ Stick to the facts when you can, avoid opinion
- ☐ Thank others who share with you
- ☐ Credit others with information they share with you that you pass on
- ☐ Strive to exceed expectations, e.g., give more than is required
- ☐ Implement process to ensure that all collaborators have an opportunity to share
- ☐ Set ground rules for communication in collaboration settings
- ☐ Invite varied opinions and discussion – disagreement is sometimes a good thing
- ☐ Encourage wild ideas, creativity and innovation
- ☐ Create a psychologically safe environment where others feel free to speak
- ☐ Maintain confidentiality where applicable

Masotti Commonsense Social Competence Strategy #9– Be Hardy

- ☐ Anticipate and plan for a physically demanding environment, e.g., consider what you and/or your team need to work well related to:
    - Noise
    - Deadlines
    - Moving equipment
    - Moving vehicles
    - Ventilation: quality and noise associated with
    - Repetitive motion
    - Safety equipment e.g., that hinders movement
    - Physical barriers to communication
    - Tight spaces
    - Large, open spaces
    - Difficulty related to equipment
    - Range of motion required
    - Time standing
    - Distance to areas you need to go to on the job, e.g., parking to work site
    - Availability of washrooms
    - Allowable breaks
    - Allergens
    - Chemicals
    - General morale
    - Temperature in the room
    - Availability of food and water
    - Availability of first aid or emergency equipment
- ☐ Take care of your personal needs:
    - Sleep when you can and for a reasonable amount of time
    - Keep up with regular body maintenance: dentist, eye doctor, doctor
    - Have supply of any required medications on hand
    - Exercise regularly
    - Eat a healthy diet
    - Practice effective stress management
    - Practice good hygiene, e.g., hair, nails, shaving,

etc.
- Make it a habit to keep clothes clean and in good repair
- Maintain safety standards, e.g., wear safety equipment
- Watch for typical "look and behaviour" when you/or others are doing the job. If there is variance, or off-standard look and behaviour, consider if that behaviour is impacting performance. If it is, you need to address what you are seeing.
  - You don't need to know the reason, you just identify and call out the behaviour e.g., to prevent an injury, etc.
  - Ask questions to discover cause of off-standard behaviour, e.g., due to:
    - ☐ Drugs
    - ☐ Alcohol
    - ☐ Nervous breakdown
    - ☐ High stress
    - ☐ External situation, e.g., personal trauma
    - ☐ Illness
    - ☐ Depression
    - ☐ Hunger
    - ☐ Exhaustion
    - ☐ Distress

Masotti Commonsense Social Competence Strategy #10 – Be Responsible

- Run your own race: Decide what you want out of life and make a plan to achieve it.
- Establish personal standards e.g.,
  - Morning routing
  - Daily exercise
  - Eat healthy

- - Only take jobs that pay minimum of X
  - Do not engage in, or endorse, illegal activity
  - Pay what I owe
- Establish personal policies, e.g.,
  - Do not lie
  - Always do more than is expected
  - Always consider how my actions will impact others
  - Never steal
  - Always save someone else some hardship or misery if I can
  - Give without expecting anything in return
- Clarify expectations of others
- Make promises, but only if you can keep them
- Learn to say no
- Learn to apologize
- Accept compliments
- Accept apologies from others
- Invite feedback
- Learn from mistakes
- Forgive yourself for mistakes
- Accept that you can't fix/help/save everyone; people have to learn to take responsibility for themselves
- Be sure you know what your specific responsibilities are, e.g., job tasks
- Take ownership of our own learning

Made in the USA
Columbia, SC
27 February 2020